Thru the First Disciple's Eyes

Thru The First Disciple's Eyes, Volume 1

John H Brennan

Published by John H Brennan, 2023.

While every precaution has been taken in the preparation of this book, the publisher assumes no responsibility for errors or omissions, or for damages resulting from the use of the information contained herein.

THRU THE FIRST DISCIPLE'S EYES

First edition. March 18, 2023.

Copyright © 2023 John H Brennan.

ISBN: 979-8215549506

Written by John H Brennan.

To my lovely and caring wife, Theresa. Her every day actions made it so easy to write about the wonderful nature and characteristics of the Blessed Mother Mary.

Introduction

Thru the First Disciple's Eyes is a groundbreaking exploration of the life and teachings of Jesus Christ from the perspective of his true first disciple, Mary, the mother of Jesus. This book challenges traditional views of Mary as a passive figure in the story of Jesus, and instead presents Her as an active participant in His ministry, a powerful spiritual leader, and a woman of great courage, wisdom and strength.

For centuries, Mary has been portrayed as a passive, meek figure in the story of Jesus, a symbol of obedience and humility rather than a true disciple. However, recent scholarship and theological reflection have begun to challenge this traditional view of Mary, and to recognize her as a powerful figure in her own right.

Thru the First Disciple's Eyes builds on this emerging understanding of Mary and presents a bold new vision of her role in the life and ministry of Jesus. Drawing on a range of historical and literary sources, as well as theological reflection and personal insight, this book offers a fresh and compelling perspective on the life and teachings of Jesus, and on the spiritual journey of all those who seek to follow him.

The book, Part One of the Series, is divided into simple chapters, each exploring a different aspect of Mary's life and ministry. Beginning with the first chapter, "The Invitation," focuses on Mary's remarkable encounter with the angel Gabriel, traditionally referred to as Mary's Annunciation, her acceptance of God's call to be the mother of Jesus, which truly was an invitation. Her acceptance of the invitation Gabriel delivered was not a given. The young woman Mary was betrothed to Joseph, but also known to him as wanting to remain as a virgin. A sudden pregnancy was something that could have turned disastrous for Mary, but she demonstrated true faith and courage in God's Plan and said yes. Our journey with Mary through the highlights of her son's life to Bethlehem, to Egypt, back to Nazareth, to the Jordan River, and several other locations, and finally to Jerusalem to complete His mission. Through Mary's eyes, we gain a new appreciation for the profound spiritual significance of the Incarnation, and for the deep faith and courage required to say "yes" to God's call.

We explore Mary's role as the mother of Jesus, and the challenges she faced in raising and supporting her son as he embarked on his mission. Through Mary's eyes, we gain a new appreciation for the complexities of family life, and for the ways in which Mary's own journey of faith was intertwined with that of her son.

Through Mary's eyes, we see Jesus as a teacher and healer, and we witness the powerful impact he had on those around him. Mary emerges as a key figure in this story, offering her own insights and wisdom, and helping to shape the message of Jesus for generations to come.

Throughout "Thru the First Disciple's Eyes", Mary emerges as a deeply spiritual figure, a woman of great faith and wisdom, and a true disciple of Jesus. By presenting the life and teachings of Jesus from her perspective, this book offers a powerful and transformative vision of Christianity, one that invites us all to see the world through the eyes of the first disciple, and maybe accept the role of discipleship ourselves.

The next book of the series, Part Two, "The Discipleship Continues," explores Mary's role as a disciple of Jesus, accompanying John on his ministry to Ephesus and beyond.

The Invitation

The morning sun was just starting to rise above the hills of Nazareth as she noticed the ceiling of her room illuminate. Mary rubbed the sleep from her eyes as she stretched her arms and took a deep breath of the cool morning air. The gentle chirping of the birds and the distant sound of sheep bleating in the fields filled her ears as she climbed on the chair to close the window of her room.

The warm aroma of freshly baked bread filled her nostrils, making her stomach growl with hunger. Mary's mother, Anne, greeted her with a warm smile and handed her a bowl of steaming hot porridge, topped with honey and nuts. Mary eagerly dug into her breakfast, relishing the sweet and nutty flavor that filled her mouth with every bite.

After breakfast, Mary recited the Birkat Ha-Mazon with her mom, thanking God for the food and blessings he had bestowed upon her and her family. She then proceeded to help her mom with the household chores, sweeping the floor and tidying up the small living space. As she worked, Mary chatted with her mother about the latest gossip in town, giggling at some of the more scandalous stories.

Once the chores were finished, Mary dashed outside to meet her two best friends, Rachel and Hannah. The three girls skipped rope in the sunshine, giggling and singing songs as they jumped and twirled. Mary's heart swelled with happiness as she watched the sun glint off Rachel's golden curls and felt the warm breeze ruffle her own long, dark hair.

As the morning wore on, the girls grew tired and thirsty, and decided to head back inside for a mid-morning snack. Anne had prepared a platter of fresh figs and grapes, which the girls eagerly devoured, washing the sweet fruit down with cool, clear water.

After their snack, Mary and her friends joined Anne in the small prayer room, where they recited the mid-day prayer, thanking God for his love and guidance. Mary felt a sense of calm wash over her as she spoke the familiar words, feeling the weight of the day's worries lift from her shoulders.

As the sun rose high in the sky, Mary, Hannah and Rachel walked down the road to pick up some fresh vegetables from Esther, a woman who had a small stand. Esther's husband farmed the small plot of land they owned and were often very generous with their crops with Anne and Joachim. Mary brought three eggs from her chickens with her to give Esther for the small bag of vegetables. Rachel suggested that Mary and Hannah come to her house, just a short distance beyond Esther's house where they could play tag, as there were many more places to hide than at Mary's house.

By midafternoon, Mary remembered that her mom needed the onions from Esther's farm to make dinner, so she told Rachel and Hannah she had to go home. When she was about half way home, the wind picked up, lifting the dry dust from the road in the swirling wind around her. She shielded her eyes and mouth as best as she could with her hands. Just as quickly as the wind stirred, it stopped. As Mary lowered her hands from her face, she was stunned to see a bright light shining around her. She was filled with fear and confusion, not knowing what was happening. She could make out the profile of someone in the bright light walking toward her. And then, he spoke to her, his name was Gabriel. His face shining with a divine light, his words filled her with shock and awe.

"Mary, do not be afraid, for you have found favor with God," the he said. He told Mary that she was full of grace. She didn't understand what Gabriel was saying to her. He said that God knew that she was promised in marriage to Joseph, but God had sent him to ask her a very important question. The angel told Mary that she would have a son, whom she was to name Jesus. The angel said, "He will be great and will be called the Son of the Most High God."

Mary said "how this could be as I am still a virgin". The angel answered, "The Holy Spirit will come on you, and God's power will rest on you". She couldn't believe what she was hearing. She thought to herself "Why had God chosen me, a simple girl from Nazareth, to be the mother of his Son?" She felt overwhelmed by the weight of this responsibility, and she didn't know if she was ready for it.

He also told Mary that her much older cousin Elizabeth was six months pregnant, for there is nothing that God cannot do. With a gentle and reassuring voice, he told her that she had been chosen because of her faith and devotion to God, and that he would be with her every step of the way. Mary replied, "I am the Lord's servant, let it be done according to His Will".

Mary felt a sense of peace wash over her. She knew that she could trust in God's plan, and that he would give her the strength and courage to fulfill the incredible task that he had given her.

And so, She said yes to God's plan, and from that moment on, her life was forever changed. Mary knew that she would face challenges and difficulties, but she also knew that God was with her, guiding her every step of the way.

As for her, she will always cherish the moment when the archangel Gabriel appeared to her in Nazareth, and told her that she had found favor with God. It was a moment of divine revelation, one that filled her with both fear and awe.

As she reflected on that moment, she realized that it was a turning point in her life. It was the moment when she fully embraced God's plan for her, and surrendered her life to his will. It was also a moment of great humility, as she realized that she was not in control of her life, but that God was the one who held her future in his hands.

But it was also a moment of great joy, as Mary realized that God's love for her was greater than anything she could ever imagine. And as she carried Jesus in her womb, She felt a sense of purpose and fulfillment that she had never felt before.

She continued on home, full of wonder and amazement at what had just happened. She shared the news with her mom and dad, who were as surprised as She was. And then, She spent the rest of the day in prayer, seeking guidance and strength from God.

Pregnancy

Mary's heart was filled with both excitement and fear as she gazed down at the small bump that had formed just below her belly button. It had only been a few weeks since she had received the news of her pregnancy, but it felt like a lifetime had passed. She couldn't help but feel grateful and humbled that God had chosen her to be the mother of His son, but at the same time, she was acutely aware of the danger and social stigmatization that came with being an unwed mother.

As she sat alone in her room, Mary's mind raced with thoughts of what was to come. Would Joseph still marry her? Would her family accept her and her child, or would they cast her out? These questions weighed heavily on her mind, but despite her fears, Mary felt an overwhelming sense of peace knowing that she was doing God's will.

The days that followed were filled with both joy and pain as Mary's body began to adjust to the changes brought on by her pregnancy. The nausea and fatigue that came with the first trimester made it difficult for her to keep up with her daily routine, but she was determined to do her best.

Despite her struggles, Mary felt a deep sense of gratitude towards God for choosing her to carry His son. She often found herself reciting the words of her Magnificat, praising God for the great things He had done for her and for all of Israel. She knew that her pregnancy was not just about her but was part of a much larger plan that had been prophesied centuries before.

The words of Isaiah 7:14, which had been passed down through generations, echoed in her mind, "Therefore the Lord himself will give you a sign: The virgin will conceive and give birth to a son, and will call him Immanuel." Mary knew that she was that virgin, and that her son would be the long-awaited Messiah.

As Mary's pregnancy progressed, she began to feel a deep sense of connection with her unborn child. She would often place her hand on her belly and speak to him, telling him how much she loved him and how she couldn't wait to hold him in her arms. It was during these moments that she felt closest to God, knowing that He was with her and her child every step of the way.

But as much as Mary cherished these moments, she also knew that her pregnancy put her in great danger. Unwed mothers were often ostracized and shamed in her community, and some were even stoned to death for their perceived transgressions. Mary knew that she was not immune to these dangers and that her life, as well as her child's, was at risk.

Despite these dangers, Mary remained steadfast in her faith, knowing that God would protect her and her child. She clung to the words of Micah 5:2-5, which spoke of a ruler who would come from Bethlehem and would bring peace and justice to the land. She knew that her child was that ruler and that he would change the world.

As Mary approached the end of her first trimester, she was filled with a mix of emotions. On one hand, she was excited to meet her child and to see what great things he would accomplish. But on the other hand, she was afraid of what the future held for her and her child. Would they be accepted or rejected by their community? Would they be able to fulfill God's plan for their lives?

Despite her fears, Mary remained grateful and humble, knowing that everything that was happening to her was part of God's plan. She continued to recite her Magnificat, praising God for all that He had done and all that He would do in the future. And as she looked down at her growing bump, she knew that her child was not just hers, but was also God's, and that He would guide and protect them every step of the way.

As Mary's pregnancy became more apparent, she knew that she couldn't keep it a secret any longer. She had to tell Joseph and her family, even if it meant facing their judgment and possible rejection. One day, with a heavy heart, Mary approached Joseph and shared the news of her pregnancy with him. She feared that he would be angry or upset with her, but to her surprise, he listened attentively and was filled with compassion and understanding. She knew it would be a journey of faith, humility, and gratitude, and it would continue to teach her that with God, all things are possible.

Joseph knew that Mary was a virtuous and faithful woman, and he believed that her pregnancy was a miracle from God. He pledged to stand by her side and to raise their child together, no matter what the world might say. With Joseph's support, Mary found the courage to tell her family, who also listened with compassion and understanding. They welcomed her with open arms and vowed to support her and her child, no matter what the cost.

Mary was feeling a mix of excitement and nervousness about her own pregnancy. However, she couldn't shake off the thought of her much older cousin Elizabeth, who was entering her third trimester and was due to give birth soon. Mary knew that Elizabeth needed help and support during this time, and she was determined to be there for her.

Despite the distance, Mary made the decision to travel to Elizabeth's house, which was a couple of days away. She knew it wouldn't be easy, but she felt that it was the right thing to do. She spent weeks preparing for the journey, packing all the essentials she would need and making arrangements for her own pregnancy care while she was away.

Visit to Elizabeth

Mary walked down the dirt path, the wind whispering through her hair. Her heart beat with excitement as she thought of seeing her relative Elizabeth. It had been months since she last saw her, and so much had happened since then. When Mary finally arrived at Elizabeth's house, she was relieved to see that her cousin was doing well. Mary was overjoyed to see her cousin Elizabeth. It had been a long and arduous journey for the young girl, but she had managed to make it safely to her relative's home.

Mary had been visited by an angel, who told her that she would give birth to the Son of God. She had been frightened at first, but then filled with a sense of awe and wonder. Now, being at Elizabeth's home, she felt a new sense of peace. Elizabeth's greeting was warm and genuine, and Mary felt a sense of comfort in the older woman's presence.

Elizabeth greeted Mary with a warm hug, her round belly pressing against her. Mary smiled, knowing that Elizabeth was also carrying a miracle child. The angel had told her the news that Elizabeth was pregnant with John the Baptist, and it filled her heart with joy.

They sat together on a bench outside, the sun shining down on them. Mary marveled at the beauty of the countryside around them. She and Elizabeth talked about their pregnancies, and how excited they were to have their sons grow up together.

"I can hardly believe it," Elizabeth said, her eyes shining. "To think that both of our sons will be born under such miraculous circumstances."

Mary nodded, her hand resting on her own belly. "I feel blessed beyond measure," she said softly. "To be chosen to carry the Son of God...it is a great honor."

They talked for hours, catching up on old times and sharing their hopes and dreams for the future. Mary told Elizabeth about the angel who had visited her, and Elizabeth listened with rapt attention.

"It is truly a miracle," Elizabeth said, tears in her eyes. "God works in mysterious ways."

Mary nodded, a sense of peace filling her heart. She knew that God was with her, guiding her every step of the way.

As the day wore on, they went inside and prepared a meal together. Mary helped chop vegetables while Elizabeth cooked the meat. They laughed and talked as they worked, their joy infectious.

When the meal was ready, they sat down to eat, the aroma of food filling the room. They gave thanks to God for the blessings they had received, and for the miracle of their pregnancies.

After dinner, they sat together on the porch, watching the sunset. Mary felt a deep sense of contentment, as if everything in the world was right.

As the night fell, Elizabeth led Mary to a small room in the back of the house. "This will be your room," she said, smiling. "I hope you find it comfortable."

Mary thanked her and settled in, the soft blanket and pillow comforting her tired body. She felt the baby move inside her, a reminder of the miracle growing within her.

As she drifted off to sleep, she felt a deep sense of peace. She knew that God was with her, guiding her every step of the way. And she knew that she was not alone, that Elizabeth was there to support her through the coming months.

Over the next few weeks, Mary devoted herself to helping Elizabeth in any way she could, from cooking and cleaning to walking to the market for fresh food. She also shared her own experiences of pregnancy with Elizabeth, getting her advice and providing a listening ear whenever she needed it. In the end, Mary's decision to travel to Elizabeth's house.

A week after John the Baptist was born, Mary and Elizabeth said their goodbyes, promising to keep in touch. Mary felt a sense of sadness as she left, knowing that she would miss Elizabeth and the peaceful countryside around her.

As She left, She knew that she was blessed beyond measure, and that the future held great promise. And she knew that, no matter what happened, she would always carry the miracle of her pregnancy with her, a reminder of God's love and grace. But she also felt a sense of excitement, knowing that she was carrying the Son of God within her. She knew that she had a great responsibility, but she also knew that she was not alone. God was with her, and the Spirit was guiding her every step of the way.

Trip to Bethlehem and Jesus' Birth:

Mary trudged along the dusty, rocky road, her swollen feet aching with every step. She had been on the journey from Nazareth to Bethlehem for over a week now, and the rugged terrain and scorching sun were taking their toll on her weary body. As she rode on the back of a donkey, she tried to focus on the rhythmic swaying of its gait to keep her mind off the pains that wracked her. She could feel the baby inside her, kicking and squirming, as if sensing the hardship of the journey.

They had left Nazareth with hope in their hearts, Joseph leading the way with a confident stride. But as they progressed, the road became more treacherous and the weather more unforgiving. Mary had not expected the journey to be easy, but she had not anticipated the extent of the hardship that awaited her.

When Joseph and Mary entered the bustling market town Shechem (you may now know it as Nablus), they recalled how this was the town where our ancestors arrived from Egypt, first led by Moses. The irony of their trip to Israel from Egypt to escape the Pharaoh would not be known for a couple months when Joseph would bring our son and me to Egypt to escape Herod.

She couldn't help but take in the rich aromas that surrounded me. The warm, yeasty fragrance of freshly baked bread wafted through the air, tempting she senses with its comforting scent. The smell of olives, both briny and earthy, was also prominent, reminding me of the delicious dishes that could be made with this versatile fruit.

But it was the sweet, sticky scent of figs that truly caught her attention. The ripe fruit, plucked fresh from nearby trees, brought back memories of home and family. She imagined herself sitting under the shade of a fig tree, sharing this delicious treat with loved ones. The scent of figs was unique, a perfect combination of sweetness and earthiness that was hard to resist.

As they shared these traditional foods with other visitors, they felt a sense of community and belonging. The smells of olives, figs, and bread were a testament to the richness and diversity of Middle Eastern cuisine, and a reminder of the power of food to bring people together. The scent of these foods would forever be etched in she memory as a part of this journey, evoking both joy and longing for the comforts of home. But they knew they would have to leave in the morning.

The first few days had been manageable, with Joseph making sure they had enough food and water to last them the journey. But as they approached the end of their journey, supplies became scarce and Mary felt her hunger and thirst grow more insistent. The sun beat down on her relentlessly, and she had to shield her face from its harsh glare with a makeshift scarf. The dust that rose with every step made it difficult to breathe, and Mary felt as if she was inhaling sand.

Joseph was doing his best to keep her comfortable, but even he was struggling to cope with the demands of the journey. His face was creased with worry, and Mary could see that he was becoming increasingly anxious about her condition. She knew that the baby could come at any moment, and the thought of giving birth in the middle of nowhere terrified her.

As night fell, they found a sheltered spot to camp, and Joseph set about preparing a fire and some meager rations. Mary sat huddled by the fire, her stomach growling with hunger, and her mind drifting to thoughts of home. She missed her mother, and her friends, and the familiar streets of Nazareth. She longed for the comfort of her own bed and the sound of her mother's voice.

But there was no turning back now. The journey had to be completed, and the baby had to be born. Mary knew that she had to be strong, for herself, for Joseph, and for the child that was about to come into the world.

The next few days were a blur of pain and exhaustion. Mary's contractions grew stronger, and she had to stop every few minutes to catch her breath. Joseph was doing his best to keep her moving, but even he was struggling with the weight of her body on the back of the donkey. Mary could feel the sweat pouring down her face, and the tears streaming down her cheeks. She was in agony, but she knew that she had to keep going.

Finally, they arrived at Bethlehem, exhausted and depleted. Yet Mary's heart was filled with a deep sense of gratitude and joy. She was grateful for the love of her husband, for the journey they had taken together, and for the promise of a new life that lay before them. The streets were crowded with people, and Mary could feel the stares of strangers as they passed by. She knew that they were looking at her belly, wondering who she was, and what she was doing in their town.

Joseph led her to a stable at the edge of the town, and they set about making a makeshift bed from straw and blankets. Mary lay down, her body wracked with pain, and she knew that the moment of birth was near. Mary felt a sense of anticipation rising within her. This was the city of David, the place where her son would be born.

As she pushed and strained, Mary felt a sense of wonder and awe at the miracle of birth. She thought about the child she was bringing into the world, about the promise that he held, and about the love that she and Joseph would pour into his life.

As the baby emerged, Mary felt a wave of relief wash over her. The pain had been worth it, for this tiny, perfect creature that had entered her life. She held the baby to her chest, marveling at his tiny fingers and toes, and the sound of his cries as he took his first breaths of life. Mary held him close, tears streaming down her face as she looked into his tiny face. He was perfect and beautiful, with a halo of golden hair and deep blue eyes.

As she wrapped him in swaddling clothes, Mary felt a sense of overwhelming love and protectiveness. This child was hers, and she would do anything to keep him safe.

Shepherds and Sheep

Mary had been awake for what felt like an eternity, and yet she still could not believe what had just happened. She was holding her newborn son, Jesus, close to her chest, as she and Joseph lay huddled together in a makeshift stable.

As she gazed down at her baby, she was overcome with emotions: joy, wonder, and a deep sense of gratitude to God for blessing her with this precious gift.

But as she was lost in her thoughts, a commotion outside the stable suddenly interrupted her reverie. She heard the sound of voices, loud and boisterous, accompanied by the unmistakable bleating of sheep.

Mary's heart quickened as she realized that they were being visited by shepherds. She had heard about them before - rough, uneducated men who tended to their flocks in the fields outside of town.

She could not help but feel a sense of apprehension. How would they react to her, Joseph, and the baby? Would they be frightened, or perhaps even hostile?

As the voices grew louder, Joseph quickly rose to his feet, taking a defensive stance in front of Mary and Jesus. But to their surprise, the shepherds did not seem to be a threat at all. In fact, they appeared to be filled with a sense of wonder and awe, as if they had just witnessed a miracle.

As they entered the stable, Mary could see the dirt and sweat on their faces, and the rough wool of their clothing. She could smell the unmistakable aroma of sheep that clung to their skin and clothing. But despite their rough exterior, there was something different about them - a sense of reverence and humility that seemed to emanate from within.

The shepherds fell to their knees before Mary and Joseph, their eyes fixed on the baby in her arms. They began to speak excitedly, their words tumbling over one another in their haste to convey what they had seen.

"We were out in the fields," one of them said, "watching our sheep when suddenly the sky lit up with a brilliant light. At first, we were afraid, but then we heard the voice of an angel, telling us not to be afraid, but to go and see the newborn Savior who had just been born in Bethlehem."

Mary listened in amazement, as the shepherds recounted their tale. She could hardly believe what she was hearing - that these rough, uneducated men had been chosen by God to witness the birth of her son.

As she gazed down at Jesus, she felt a sense of humility wash over her. She was reminded that God uses all people, regardless of their class or status, to demonstrate his love for humanity.

Mary realized that this was the true message of her son's birth - that God's love was not reserved for the wealthy, the powerful, or the educated, but for all people, regardless of their background. In that moment, she felt a deep sense of compassion for the shepherds, knowing that they had been chosen by God to witness something truly miraculous.

Mary welcomed the shepherds into the stable, offering them a place to rest and refresh themselves. She could see the exhaustion etched on their faces, the weariness that came from a life spent tending to their flocks in the fields.

As she sat with them, she realized that they were not so different from her and Joseph. They were all travelers on the same journey, all seeking to understand God's love and purpose for their lives.

Despite the differences in their circumstances, Mary knew that they were all united by a common bond - a love for God that transcended all boundaries.

Mary and Joseph sat on a small blanket spread on the ground, surrounded by the shepherds who had come to visit them. In front of them lay a simple spread of bread, cheese, and fruit, which they shared with their guests. The sounds of the gentle wind rustling through the trees mingled with the bleating of nearby sheep and the cooing of baby Jesus.

As they ate, Mary and Joseph couldn't help but feel a deep sense of gratitude for the shepherds who had come to visit them. These humble men had been the first to hear the news of Jesus' birth, and they had come to see the newborn King with their own eyes. Mary watched as Joseph broke off a piece of bread and offered it to one of the shepherds, a gesture of hospitality that was typical of their culture.

As they shared the simple meal, the animals that surrounded them stood perfectly still, their eyes fixed on the newborn baby in Mary's arms. The sheep that had been grazing nearby had gathered around the small group, their woolly bodies creating a warm, protective circle around them.

Despite the simplicity of their surroundings, Mary and Joseph felt an overwhelming sense of peace and contentment. They knew that their lives would never be the same again, now that they had been blessed with the gift of their son, Jesus. As they sat there, sharing bread, cheese, and fruit with their new friends, they were filled with a deep sense of joy and gratitude for the beauty of the moment they were sharing.

As the shepherds prepared to depart, they were filled with a sense of joy and wonder that would stay with them for the rest of their lives.

They had witnessed something truly miraculous, and they knew that their lives would never be the same again.

Mary watched as they left the stable, their forms silhouetted against the night sky. She knew that they would spread the word of her son's birth, that they would tell others of the miracle that they had witnessed.

And as she watched them go, she felt a sense of peace wash over her. She knew that her son had been born for a purpose, that he had come to bring hope and salvation to all people.

She realized that this message of hope and love was something that could unite all people, regardless of their background or station in life. And she knew that it was up to each person to embrace this message, to live their lives in a way that demonstrated God's love and compassion for all people.

As she gazed down at her son, she was filled with a sense of gratitude and humility. She knew that she had been chosen for a great task, that she had been entrusted with a responsibility that was greater than anything she could have ever imagined.

But she also knew that this responsibility was not hers alone. She was part of a greater story, a story that included all people, from the lowliest shepherd to the mightiest king.

And so, Mary held her son close, knowing that he was a symbol of hope and love for all people. She knew that his birth was not just a miracle, but a message - a message that would inspire all people to live their lives with compassion, kindness, and love for one another. As they watched him grow, Mary and Joseph knew that he was no ordinary child. They could see the light of God shining in his eyes, and they knew that he was destined for great things.

The Presentation

Mary stood outside the entrance of the Temple, her heart pounding in her chest. She clutched tightly to the swaddled bundle in her arms, her eyes scanning the crowds that bustled past her. She had waited for this moment for what felt like an eternity, and now that it was here, she was filled with a mix of excitement and trepidation.

She looked down at the tiny face of her newborn son, Jesus. He was sleeping soundly, completely unaware of the significance of the moment. Mary took a deep breath and stepped forward, following her husband Joseph into the bustling crowds.

As they made their way through the Temple gates, Mary felt a sudden sense of awe wash over her. The air was thick with the scent of incense, and the walls were adorned with intricate carvings and golden ornaments. The sound of singing echoed through the halls, filling Mary's heart with joy.

They were led to a room where an old man was waiting for them. His name was Simeon, and he was known throughout the Temple for his wisdom and his devotion to God. He approached Mary and Joseph with a gentle smile, his eyes fixed on the sleeping child in Mary's arms.

"Welcome, my friends," he said, his voice soft and gentle. "I have been waiting for you."

Mary felt a lump form in her throat as Simeon took the baby Jesus from her arms. She watched as he cradled her son in his arms, his eyes closed in prayer.

"Lord, now let your servant depart in peace, according to your word," Simeon said. "For my eyes have seen your salvation, which you have prepared in the presence of all peoples."

Mary felt a sudden surge of emotion as she watched the old man speak. She knew that her son was special, that he had been chosen by God for a great purpose. But to hear Simeon speak of it so openly was overwhelming.

Simeon turned to Mary and Joseph, his eyes gleaming with tears. "This child is destined for the falling and the rising of many in Israel, and to be a sign that will be opposed so that the inner thoughts of many will be revealed – and a sword will pierce your own soul too."

Mary felt a chill run down her spine at Simeon's words. She knew that her son's life would not be easy, that he would face opposition and hardship. But to hear it spoken so plainly was sobering.

As Simeon handed the baby back to Mary, she felt a sudden sense of relief. The weight of the moment lifted from her shoulders, and she felt a sense of peace settle over her.

But the moment was not over yet. As they turned to leave, they were approached by an old woman named Anna. She was a prophetess, known for her devotion to God and her wisdom. Anna approached Mary and Joseph with a warm smile, her eyes fixed on the baby Jesus.

"Can I hold him?" she asked.

Mary nodded, and Anna gently took the baby from her arms. She held him close, her eyes fixed on his face. "This is the one," she said softly. "This is the one we have been waiting for."

Mary felt a sudden rush of emotion as she watched Anna hold her son. She knew that he was special, that he had been chosen by God for a great purpose. But to hear it spoken so plainly was overwhelming.

As they left the Temple, Mary felt a sense of awe wash over her. She knew that her son's life would not be easy, that he would face opposition and hardship. But she also knew that he was destined for greatness, that he would change the world in ways she could never have imagined.

As they made their way home, Mary couldn't help but feel a sense of overwhelming love for her son. She cradled him in her arms, gazing down at his peaceful face.

She thought back to the moment when the angel Gabriel had appeared to her, telling her that she had been chosen to bear a son who would be the Son of God. At the time, she had been filled with fear and uncertainty, unsure of what the future would hold.

But now, as she held her son in her arms, she knew that everything would be okay. She knew that he was special, that he had been chosen by God for a great purpose.

As they arrived back at their humble, temporary home in Bethlehem, Mary knew that their lives would never be the same. She knew that her son was destined for greatness, and that she would do everything in her power to support him on his journey.

Magi

Mary had just fed her Son, and was watching over him sleeping on his mattress, when she heard a commotion outside. She peeked through the cracks in the door and saw a group of richly dressed men approaching. She told Joseph and he went out to greet them and determine what they wanted. They were carrying gifts and seemed to be following a bright star that shone in the sky above them, directly above the place where they stayed.

As they entered with Joseph, Mary was surprised to hear that they had travelled so far. They spoke a different language and had an air of foreignness about them. But as they approached her and her son, she could feel a sense of reverence and awe emanating from them.

The Magi knelt before her as she held Jesus, offering gifts of gold, frankincense, and myrrh which were rare and valuable commodities. Mary was touched by their generosity and felt a sense of gratitude for these strangers who had come so far to pay homage to her son. The scents of frankincense and myrrh, immediately filled the house with a strong, but pleasant aroma.

Joseph asked that they stay and offered them a simple meal of bread and olives and some other local foods. As they spoke to them, Mary and Joseph could sense that these men were wise and learned, and they listened carefully as they shared their knowledge of the stars and prophecies that had led them to Bethlehem, also known as the House of Bread. Mary could feel a sense of wonder and awe building within her as they spoke, and she couldn't help but feel that there was something special about her son, something that went beyond the ordinary.

Joseph told them they had travelled to Bethlehem a few short weeks earlier from Nazareth, Mary's hometown but said that he was originally from Bethlehem. Joseph continued that they traveled to Bethlehem for the census because he belonged to the house and line of David. King David was also from Bethlehem.

The magi talked of the alignment of the stars over Bethlehem indicated a great king would come from another great king. This is what caused them to leave their homes for whatever lands the stars would bring them.

After they had finished speaking, the Magi took their leave, promising to return to their countries with news of what they had discovered. Mary watched them go, feeling a sense of peace and joy fill her heart.

Over the next few days, as Mary rested and cared for her son, she couldn't help but reflect on the events that had taken place. She felt grateful for the Magi and their visit, knowing that they had recognized something special in her son. She also felt a sense of astonishment, knowing that there was much she still didn't understand about what being the mother of Jesus would mean.

She just closed her eyes and let herself sink into the moment, feeling the gentle rhythm of her son's breathing and the warmth of his body against hers. And as she did, she felt a sense of gratitude and awe wash over her, knowing that she had been chosen to play a part in the divine plan of salvation.

Mary had drifted off to sleep, waking a few hours later in the Grotto, holding her sleeping son close to her chest. She was filled with sense of peace and contentment. The room was still filled with the scents of the spices the magi brought. A soft, warm light was present, and the walls appeared to display images of angels dancing with the soft sounds of prayer and song drifting in from the nearby temple, and she felt a deep sense of connection to the divine. She realized the soft glow was emanating from her son's face. The light was not coming from the oil lamp that illuminated the room, nor was it from the flickering candles. It was a light that was flow from within her infant.

But for now, she was content to sit in the quiet, holding her son close and feeling the presence of the divine all around her. She knew that the journey ahead would not be easy, but she also knew that she was not alone, with Joseph at her side, the Holy Spirit would continue to guide her on her path. And with that knowledge, she closed her eyes and offered a silent prayer of thanks, knowing that she had been blessed in ways she could not fully comprehend.

Mary held her breath, not wanting to disturb the peaceful slumber of her child as she placed him on the mat. The dim light in the room grew brighter... she realized that something extraordinary was happening. Suddenly, the room was totally filled with a bright, blinding light, and Mary felt herself being lifted up, as if on wings.

She looked down and saw her sleeping son, but now he was surrounded by a host of angels, their wings spread wide and their voices raised in song. Mary watched in wonder as the angels lifted her up into the air and carried her out of the room, leaving him behind. One of the angels said, "Mary, do not worry about him right now. There are an entire league of angels keeping him safe while we are on this journey".

At first, Mary was frightened. She had never experienced anything like this before, and she didn't know what was happening. But then she felt a sense of peace wash over her, and she knew that she was in the hands of the divine.

She closed her eyes and let herself be carried along by the angels, feeling the wind rushing past her and the warmth of their bodies against hers. And as she did, she felt a sense of awe and wonder wash over her, knowing that she was witnessing something truly extraordinary. They soared into the sky, higher and higher, until they were high above the earth.

Mary gazed down, and to her amazement, she saw a world filled with peace and harmony. People of every nation, tribe, and tongue lived together in perfect harmony. They worked, played, and worshipped together, sharing everything they had with one another.

The angels pointed out different parts of the world, showing Mary the beauty and harmony that existed in each place. In one region, she saw children laughing and playing in the streets, while their parents worked together to build a new community center. In another, she saw farmers working side by side, planting and harvesting crops that would feed their entire village.

As they flew over the world, the angels also showed Mary the suffering that would exist if it weren't for the sacrifice that her son would make. She saw people dying from disease, famine, and war. She saw families torn apart by greed and hatred, and individuals consumed by fear and despair.

But amidst the suffering, she also witnessed the power of love and compassion. She saw those who had chosen to follow in Jesus' footsteps, living lives of service and sacrifice, bringing hope and healing to those around them. She saw families and communities coming together, sharing their resources and their lives with one another.

The angels spoke to Mary, telling her that her son's mission was to bring light to a dark world, to show people the way to true life and hope and focus on their eternal life. They told her that his life would be filled with hardship and pain, but that his sacrifice would ultimately bring redemption and restoration to all of creation.

Mary felt her heart breaking as she thought of the trials that her son would endure. But she also felt a glimmer of hope and strength. She knew that her son was not alone, that he was surrounded by a host of angels and the prayers of all who loved him.

As the angels carried her and her son back to earth, Mary felt a renewed sense of purpose and determination. She knew that the road ahead would not be easy, but she also knew that she had been given a great gift, a vision of the future.

As they flew over the rooftops of Bethlehem, Mary saw the world in a new light. She saw the beauty and wonder of creation, the intricate web of life that linked all beings together, and the deep sense of love and compassion that lay at the heart of all things. Yet, she also had seen the weakness of the human heart to seek love in the things of this world, not the next.

And as they approached the grotto, the angels lowered her back to her chair and slowly lowered her son onto her lap. The wind swirled thru the house like the day Gabriel visited her, so she hastily covered the baby and her face with her mantle until the wind left them. She pulled back her veil to see Joseph standing over them and said, "Mary, I just had a dream. We must pack our things and leave right away. Herod wants to kill Jesus."

Egypt?

"Yes, we need to leave, Mary," Joseph replied, his voice low and urgent. "We have to go to Egypt."

Egypt? Mary had never been to Egypt before. She had heard stories of the great pyramids and the Nile river, but she had never even dreamed of going there. And why did they need to go there now? She looked at Joseph, her eyes wide with confusion and concern.

"What's going on, Joseph?" she asked, her voice trembling slightly.

"I had a dream," Joseph replied, his voice still low. "An angel appeared to me in the dream and told me that King Herod is looking for Jesus. He wants to kill him."

Mary gasped, her hand flying up to her mouth. Kill Jesus? The very thought made her heart ache with fear and sadness. She held her son closer to her chest, as if she could protect him from harm just by holding him tight.

"What do we do?" she asked, her voice shaking.

"We have to leave, Mary," Joseph said, his eyes pleading with her. "We have to go to Egypt. It's the only way to keep Jesus safe."

Mary knew that Joseph was right. She trusted him implicitly, knowing that he was a man of great faith and courage. She nodded, her eyes filling with tears as she tried to process what was happening.

"Okay," she whispered. "I'll pack our things."

Together, they worked quickly to gather what little they could take with them. Mary wrapped Jesus in a warm blanket and carefully placed him in a small basket, which she then secured to the back of the donkey. Joseph grabbed a few essentials - some bread, some water, a change of clothes - and packed them into a small bag.

They set out on their journey just as the first light of dawn was breaking over the horizon. Mary led the donkey, her heart heavy with worry and fear. Joseph walked alongside her, his hand resting gently on her shoulder.

They took a path that led them out of Bethlehem and through the surrounding countryside. Mary had traveled this path many times before, but today it seemed different somehow. The fields were barren and brown, the trees stripped of their leaves by the winter winds. There was a chill in the air that made Mary shiver, despite the layers of clothing she wore.

They passed by small villages and hamlets, their inhabitants going about their daily tasks with little notice of the travelers passing through. Mary couldn't help but wonder if any of them were in league with King Herod, if any of them knew who she and Joseph were and what they were carrying with them. She tried to push these thoughts aside, focusing instead on the feel of the donkey's warm breath on her hand and the sound of Joseph's steady footsteps beside her.

As they walked, Joseph told Mary more about his dream. He described the angel that appeared to him, its bright wings and soothing voice. He spoke of the urgency of their mission, of the need to protect Jesus at all costs. Mary listened intently, her heart swelling with pride and gratitude for the man she had chosen to marry.

Mary clutched tightly onto her sleeping son as she and Joseph hurriedly made their way toward Hebron. The air was filled with tension and fear as they left their home and began their journey. There were a couple families, also with babies they met on the path who had heard the news of the king's decree that all male infants in Bethlehem under the age of two were to be killed, and they knew they had to flee to protect their child.

The road to safety was long and treacherous, and the family was faced with numerous dangers along the way. Not only did they need to worry about the Romans, but they knew bandits lurked around every corner, and they had to be on high alert at all times. They kept their eyes peeled for any signs of danger and stayed off the main roads as much as possible, opting instead to take the more treacherous and isolated routes. This would also help them avoid the Romans.

As they travelled, the weather became harsh and unforgiving. The sun beat down on them relentlessly during the day, and the frigid winds cut through their clothing at night. They had little protection from the elements, and it was a constant struggle to stay warm and dry.

Food and water were scarce, and the family had to ration what little they had. Joseph would scavenge for food wherever he could find it, and they would often go days without a proper meal. Mary was always worried about the health of her son and herself, and tried to keep them both hydrated and fed as best as she could.

Despite the constant dangers and hardships, Mary tried to find solace in the beauty of the world around her. The towns they passed through were bustling with life and activity, and the sounds and smells of the marketplaces filled her senses. The sights of the colorful fabrics and spices brought a glimmer of joy to her heart, even in the darkest of times.

In Hebron, they were welcomed by a kind family who offered them a place to stay for the night. Mary was grateful for their hospitality and thanked them profusely for their generosity. The family had a well-stocked pantry, and they offered the travelers a warm meal and fresh water. It was the first time in days that they had been able to eat a proper meal, and Mary savored every bite.

The family's children were fascinated by the baby, and they played with him happily while Mary and Joseph rested. The sounds of their laughter and playful banter filled the room, and Mary couldn't help but smile at the sight of her son's joy.

The next day, they set out again on their journey, this time towards Beersheba. As they walked, Mary could hear the sounds of the animals in the fields around them. The lowing of the cows, the bleating of the sheep, and the cawing of the birds all blended together to form a symphony of life.

But the sounds of life were not the only things that Mary could hear. The sounds of danger were also present. They could hear the distant rumble of horses' hooves and the clanging of metal armor. Mary knew that they needed to keep moving, and they quickened their pace, hoping to outrun whatever danger lay ahead.

Their journey took them through Gaza, a bustling city filled with merchants and travelers. The smells of the spices and perfumes were overpowering, and Mary was fascinated by the colors and textures of the fabrics on display. But amidst the chaos and noise, Mary couldn't shake off the feeling of danger that lingered in the air.

They traveled for many days, stopping at small inns and rest stops along the way. Mary cared for Jesus, feeding him and changing him and singing lullabies to him to keep him calm. Joseph did his best to keep their spirits up, telling stories and making jokes to distract them from their worries.

The terrain gradually became more arid and rocky as they approached the border of Egypt. Mary marveled at the sight of the great desert stretching out before them, the sand dunes rising like waves in the distance. She had never seen anything like it before, and she felt a sense of awe and wonder mixed with her fear.

As they crossed the border into Egypt, they were met by a group of travelers heading in the opposite direction. They were a family of merchants, and they had a caravan of camels laden with goods. The leader of the group, a wise old man with a flowing white beard, took one look at Mary and Joseph and knew that they were refugees.

"Where are you headed?" he asked kindly, his eyes twinkling with compassion.

"Egypt," Joseph replied, his voice steady. "We're trying to escape King Herod."

The old man nodded, his expression grave. "Ah, Herod," he said. "A wicked man, indeed. May Yahweh protect you on your journey." Joseph waved and returned the blessings for safe travel to them.

With that, he and his caravan moved on, disappearing into the distance. Mary and Joseph continued on their way, grateful for the kindness of strangers.

They continued on their journey, passing through Pelusium, a city that had been ravaged by war. The buildings were in ruins, and the streets were littered with debris. Mary felt a sense of sadness and despair as she walked through the city, wondering how many lives had been lost in the conflict.

But despite the devastation, Mary also saw signs of hope. People were working to rebuild their homes and their lives, and there was a sense of resilience and determination in the air. Mary was inspired by their strength and determination, and it gave her the courage to keep going.

But more importantly, Pelusium was the gateway to freedom and safety from the grips of Herod. No longer did they need to worry about the safety of their baby, as long as they stayed away from the slaughter of the little ones in Bethlehem. Mary mourned the loss of the innocents and their moms and dads. They were victims of Herod's sinful pride, greed and insecurities.

They eventually arrived in Alexandria, the bustling port city that would be their home for the next several years. They found a small house to rent, not far from the sea. Mary was amazed by the sights and sounds of the city - the busy markets, the ships coming in and out of the harbor, the exotic foods and spices. Mary and Joseph were grateful to have found a safe haven, and they knew that they could finally rest.

As they settled into their new home, Mary couldn't help but reflect on their journey. She had been filled with fear and uncertainty, but she had also seen the beauty and resilience of the world around her. She had been forced to confront the darkest parts of humanity, but she had also seen the kindness and generosity of strangers.

Most of all, Mary had found strength and courage within herself. She had been forced to protect her son at all costs, and she had risen to the challenge. She knew that their journey was far from over, but she was ready to face whatever lay ahead.

But life in Alexandria was not easy. Mary and Joseph were strangers in a strange land, and they had to work hard to make ends meet. Joseph found work as a carpenter, but he was often paid less than he deserved because he was an outsider. Mary took in sewing and embroidery jobs, using her skill with a needle to make beautiful garments and tapestries.

They made friends with some of the other Jewish families living in the city, but they were always careful to keep a low profile. They knew that King Herod had spies everywhere, and they feared that they might be discovered at any moment.

Despite the challenges they faced, Mary and Joseph found joy in raising their son. Jesus grew and thrived under their care, his bright eyes and curious nature bringing light into their lives. They taught him to speak and to walk, to read and to write. Mary sang to him and told him stories, passing on the traditions and beliefs of their people.

Mary constantly reflected on their journey and came to realize that it had been about more than just escaping danger. She felt a sense of awe and gratitude for the way that God had protected them. Despite the difficulties they faced, Mary knew that the journey had strengthened their faith and love for each other and of God. She found comfort in the knowledge that no matter where life might take them, they would always be guided by the love and protection of their heavenly Father.

Several years passed, and they received news that King Herod died. Mary and Joseph knew that it was safe to return to Judea, but they had grown attached to their life in Egypt. They had made friends and established a home for themselves there. But when Joseph had a dream in which an angel appeared to him and told him it was time to return, they knew they had to go.

They packed their things once again and set out on the long journey back to Bethlehem. This time, the terrain was familiar to Mary, and she felt a sense of comfort in seeing the familiar hills and fields. They arrived in Bethlehem just in time for Jesus to celebrate his first Passover as a young boy.

The Search

As they walked, Joseph asked Mary if she had seen Jesus with any of their relatives. Mary shook her head, telling him that she thought he was with him and the other men. Joseph's brow furrowed as he told her that he had thought Jesus was with her. They exchanged a worried look, both realizing that they had lost track of their son.

Mary's heart was heavy with worry as she and Joseph traveled back toward Nazareth. They had been on their way home from the Passover celebration in Jerusalem when they realized that Jesus was nowhere to be found. They had assumed that he was with the rest of the family, but as the hours passed, they began to fear the worst. They had to find him, no matter what it took.

The terrain was rough and uneven, with dusty roads that seemed to go on forever. The sun was beating down on them, and Mary could feel the sweat trickling down her back. She could hear the sound of Joseph's footsteps crunching on the gravel path beside her as they walked. The smell of wildflowers mixed with the scent of animals, and Mary took comfort in the familiar smells of the countryside.

They quickened their pace, hurrying towards Jerusalem. Mary's heart was pounding in her chest as she imagined the worst. She knew that the city could be dangerous, especially for a young boy traveling alone. She tried to calm herself, reminding herself that Jesus was a smart and resourceful child. Surely, he would find his way back to them.

As they entered Jerusalem, Mary's anxiety grew. The city was busy and bustling with people, and she could feel the energy of the crowd pulsing around her. She could hear the sound of vendors calling out to potential customers, and the distant hum of music playing in the background. The smells of spices and cooking food filled her nostrils, making her mouth water.

They checked with everyone they knew, but no one had seen Jesus. Panic set in as they began to realize that they might have lost him for good. They split up, searching every street and alley, asking everyone they met if they had seen a young boy traveling alone. They agreed to meet every hour at the entrance of the temple, a centrally located location. Mary's voice was hoarse from calling out his name, her heart breaking with every passing minute.

It was late in the day as they met at the temple steps. Mary suggested they ask the temple priests to pray for them. When they walked inside, they saw several people huddled in the corner. This is when they finally found him. Mary's heart swelled with relief as she saw him talking with the teachers, his young face earnest and serious as he discussed the scriptures with them. She could see the wisdom in his eyes, and she knew then that he was meant for great things.

As they approached him, Mary's relief turned to anger. She wanted to scold him, to demand to know why he had run off without telling them. But as she looked at him, she could see that he was genuinely surprised to see them. He had been so caught up in his discussion with the teachers that he had lost track of time.

They left the city, traveling back towards Nazareth. Mary's heart was heavy with emotion as she tried to process the events of the day. She could see the guilt on Joseph's face as he walked beside her, and she knew that he was blaming himself for what had happened. She reached out to take his hand, offering him a small smile of reassurance.

As they walked, Mary took in the sights and sounds around her. The sun was starting to set, casting a warm glow over the countryside.

She could see the fields stretching out before her, dotted with sheep and cattle grazing contentedly. Her relief at his safety was still mixed with a sense of unease. She knew they had to talk to Jesus, to explain to him why they had left Jerusalem without him and why they had been so worried.

As they walked, Mary felt a knot form in her stomach. She knew they had to address why had Jesus stayed behind in the temple? What was he trying to learn?

"Jesus," she said, breaking the silence. "Why did you stay in the temple?"

Jesus looked up at her, his eyes filled with curiosity. "I was listening to the teachers and asking them questions," he replied.

He told them that he had gone to the Temple because he wanted to learn more about his Father. He had been searching for answers, and the teachers there had helped him to understand the scriptures in a way that he never had before.

Mary and Joseph exchanged a look. They knew that Jesus had always been curious about his Jewish faith, but they also knew that they hadn't done enough to satisfy his thirst for knowledge. They had always known that there was something special about him, but this was beyond anything they could have imagined. Mary felt a sense of pride swell within her, knowing that her son was destined for great things.

As they continued their journey, Mary and Joseph couldn't help but talk about what had happened. They discussed how they had lost track of Jesus, and how they had worried about him. They also talked about his discussion with the teachers in the Temple, and what it could mean for their family's future.

Mary was amazed at the depth of knowledge that Jesus had already acquired. She knew that he was wise beyond his years, but this was something else entirely. She couldn't help but wonder what other insights and revelations he would have in the years to come.

Mary took a deep breath and began to speak, sharing stories from her own upbringing and ancestry. She told him about her parents, Joachim and Anne, and how they had instilled in her a deep love and reverence for the God of their ancestors. She spoke of her own childhood, of growing up in a Jewish household and learning about the laws and traditions of their faith.

Joseph added his own stories, telling Jesus about his own family history and how his ancestors had fought to preserve their Jewish faith under Roman rule. He talked about the importance of following the commandments and living a righteous life.

As they spoke, Mary watched Jesus closely, trying to gauge his reaction. He listened intently, his eyes lighting up with understanding as they shared their stories. She could see that he was hungry for more, eager to learn everything he could about their shared heritage.

Mary knew that they had a responsibility to ensure that Jesus understood the depth and richness of their faith and the Scriptures. They had to show him that their religion was not just a set of rules and traditions, but a way of life that was rooted in their love for God and their love for each other.

As they continued their journey back to Nazareth, Mary and Joseph talked to Jesus about their hopes and dreams for him. They told him how they wanted him to be a leader in their community, a beacon of hope and love to all those around him.

They talked about the challenges that lay ahead, of the difficult path that Jesus would have to walk in order to fulfill his destiny. But they also spoke of the love and support that they would offer him every step of the way.

As they talked, Mary felt her heart fill with love and pride for her son. She knew that he was destined for greatness, that he was the chosen one of God. And she was determined to do everything in her power to support him and guide him on his path.

As they finally arrived back in Nazareth, Mary and Joseph felt a sense of peace wash over them. They knew that they would continue their best to satisfy Jesus' thirst for knowledge and to guide him on his path. They knew that he was in God's hands, and that their love and support would be with him every step of the way.

Mary hugged her son tightly, feeling a sense of gratitude and awe wash over her. She knew that their journey was far from over, but she also knew that they were ready for whatever lay ahead. Together, they would face the challenges and triumphs that awaited them, secure in the knowledge that they were guided by the love and protection of their heavenly Father.

The Waters

In the years between the death of Joseph and the start of Jesus' public ministry, Mary and her son had lived a quiet life in Nazareth. As a carpenter, Jesus had continued to work in his trade, honing his skills and possibly even teaching his younger cousins the craft. Mary, as the head of the household, had taken care of domestic tasks such as cooking, cleaning, and caring for the family.

But they had also engaged in spiritual practices together. They had prayed, studied the Scriptures, and attended synagogue, deepening their faith and their relationship with God. Mary had always been a woman of great faith, and her influence had undoubtedly played an important role in shaping Jesus' own beliefs and worldview.

As Jesus grew older, Mary had watched with pride as he began to develop a reputation as a teacher and healer. She had seen the way people were drawn to him, the way he could command a room with his words and his presence. She knew that he was destined for great things, but she also knew that his path would not be easy.

Mary and Jesus sat at the small wooden table in their home, surrounded by flickering candles that illuminated the room with a warm, golden light. Mary was making a list of supplies they would need for the journey ahead, while Jesus sharpened his knife and prepared their packs.

"We need to make sure we have enough food and water," Mary said, scanning the list she had written. "And warm clothes for the cold nights."

Jesus nodded in agreement; his eyes focused on the task at hand. Mary could see the determination in his face, and she knew that he was excited for the journey ahead. But she also knew that it would not be an easy journey. The road ahead was long, and they would have to face many dangers along the way.

As they packed their bags and prepared for the journey, Mary could feel a sense of pride and apprehension in her heart. She knew that her son was destined for great things, but she also knew that the road ahead would be fraught with challenges and obstacles. She prayed silently for his safety and protection, and for the strength and courage to face whatever lay ahead.

Finally, after several hours of preparation and a few hours' sleep, they were ready to set out. Mary and Jesus mounted their donkey, and set off into the night. The stars twinkled overhead, and the cool night air filled their lungs as they made their way through the hills and valleys of Nazareth.

As they journeyed through the night, Mary and Jesus talked about the journey ahead. They discussed the challenges they would face, the people they would meet, and the lessons they would learn. Mary offered words of encouragement and advice, while Jesus listened intently, absorbing every word.

Finally, as the first rays of dawn broke over the horizon, they arrived at the Jordan River. The air was filled with the sweet scent of blooming flowers, and the sound of the rushing river filled their ears. Mary and Jesus looked out over the river, taking in the beauty and majesty of the place.

They saw John the Baptist, Jesus' cousin, standing in the clearing with a group of travelers who had gathered to hear him preach.

John had been living in the wilderness, preaching repentance and forgiveness, and baptizing people in the Jordan River. His words had drawn the attention of many, and a small community had formed around him.

Mary and Jesus greeted John with open arms, embracing him warmly. They sat around the campfire, talking and laughing, as the sun rose higher in the sky.

As they talked, a crowd began to gather, drawn by the sound of John's preaching. They came from all around, eager to hear his message of repentance and forgiveness, and to be baptized in the Jordan River.

Mary and Jesus watched as John baptized person after person, his voice ringing out over the sound of the rushing river. Jesus was moved by the power of his words, and felt a sense of deep connection to the people who were gathered there.

Mary stood on the banks of the Jordan River, watching as her son waded into the water. She could feel the power of the moment, and the love and grace of God that surrounded them all. She felt a mixture of pride and worry, knowing that this moment marked the beginning of his public ministry.

As Jesus emerged from the water, John reached out to him and placed his hands on Jesus' head. Mary could see the look of peace and contentment on her son's face, and she knew that he had been forever changed by the experience.

As she watched, John the Baptist approached Jesus, and Mary strained to hear their conversation. She knew that John had been preaching about the coming of the Messiah, and that he had been baptizing those who sought repentance and forgiveness of sins. She wondered why Jesus was seeking the same thing, if he was acknowledging the need for repentance in his own life.

Then, Mary heard John speak the words that would echo through history: "I baptize you with water, but one who is more powerful than I is coming...He will baptize you with the Holy Spirit and fire."

Mary felt a shiver run down her spine as she watched John immerse Jesus in the water, and then saw the heavens open up and the Holy Spirit descend upon him like a dove. A voice boomed from above, declaring, "This is my Son, whom I love; with him I am well pleased."

Mary felt tears prick at her eyes as she watched her son emerge from the water, knowing that his life would never be the same again. She wondered what lay ahead for him, what challenges he would face, and whether he was ready for the journey that lay ahead.

The crowd that had gathered began to cheer and sing, their voices raised in praise and gratitude. Mary felt her heart swell with pride and love for her son, and she knew that he was destined for great things.

After the baptism, Mary and Jesus spent some time alone, walking along the banks of the Jordan River. They talked about what had just happened, and what it all meant for Jesus' future.

As they walked, Mary felt a sense of foreboding in her heart. She knew that Jesus would soon be leaving her to embark on his own journey, and that the road ahead would not be easy. She recalled the angels carrying her high into the sky to see two different worlds; one filled with love in the hope of eternal salvation, the other filled with misery, hate, war and disease because they turned their backs on Jesus and lived only for the next day.

But she also knew that he was ready for whatever lay ahead, and that he would be guided and protected by the love and grace of God.

"Jesus," she said, her voice filled with love and encouragement. "I know that the road ahead will not be easy. But I also know that you are destined for greatness, and that you have the strength and courage to face whatever challenges may come your way."

Jesus looked at his mother, a small smile on his face. "I know that, too," he said. "But it still helps to hear you say it."

Mary took a deep breath, steeling herself for what she knew would be a difficult conversation. "Jesus, there is something else that I need to say," she said, her voice low and serious. "I know that you will soon be going out into the wilderness alone, to face temptation and trials. And I want you to know that I will be praying for you every day, and that my love and support will be with you always."

Jesus nodded; his eyes filled with understanding. "I know, Mom," he said. "And I am grateful for your love and support. But I also know that this is something that I must do alone, to prove myself worthy of the mission that God has given me."

Mary felt a lump rise in her throat, and she fought back tears. She knew that Jesus was right, but it was still hard to accept that he would soon be leaving her to face the unknown.

But she also knew that he was destined for greatness, and that his mission was part of a larger plan that she could not fully understand.

Jesus nodded; his eyes focused on some distant point. "This is the beginning," he said. "The beginning of the ministry that I have been called to. The beginning of the message that I have been sent to deliver."

She knew that he was embarking on a dangerous and unpredictable journey, one that could ultimately lead to his death. But she also knew that he was driven by a deep sense of purpose, a calling that he could not ignore.

"Whatever happens," she said, placing a hand on his arm, "I will always be here for you. I will always support you, no matter what."

Jesus smiled at her, a warm and comforting expression. "I know, mom" he said. "And I will always be grateful for that."

"Go, then," she said, her voice filled with love and pride. "And know that my love and prayers will be with you always."

With that, Mary hugged her son tightly, and watched as he walked away, disappearing into the wilderness.

The Wedding

As a child, Jesus had a calmness and a wisdom that was beyond his years. Mary had watched him grow into a young man with a strength and a compassion that filled her with pride. But as she watched him move through the crowds at the wedding feast in Cana, she saw something else in him - a power that she had never seen before.

Mary had been invited to the wedding by a distant cousin, and she had brought Jesus with her. It was a festive occasion, with music and dancing and the sweet smell of flowers filling the air. She watched as her son mingled with the guests, a smile on his face and a light in his eyes.

As the night wore on, the wine began to run out. Mary watched as the servants scurried around, trying to find more. She could see the worry in the faces of the hosts, and she knew that this was a moment when something needed to be done.

She turned to Jesus and whispered, "They have no wine."

Jesus looked at her, a faint smile on his lips. "What is that to me, woman? My hour has not yet come."

Mary felt a pang of disappointment at his words, but she knew her son well. She had faith in him, and she knew that he would not disappoint her. She turned to the servants and said, "Do whatever he tells you."

Jesus looked at her again, a hint of amusement in his eyes. "OK, Mom," he said. "I'll do what you ask."

Mary watched as her son walked over to the large jars of water that were standing nearby. She could hear the murmurs of the guests as they watched him, wondering what he was going to do. She held her breath as he lifted the lid off one of the jars and scooped out a handful of water.

And then, to her amazement, he turned to the guests and said, "Take this and drink it. It is the best wine you will ever taste."

Mary watched as the servants poured the water into glasses and handed them out to the guests. She watched as the guests sipped the liquid, their eyes widening in surprise and delight. She watched as the hosts looked on in wonder, unable to believe what they were seeing.

And then she turned to her son, a sense of awe filling her heart. She knew then that he was not just a man, but something more - something divine. She knew that he was the one who had been sent to save them all.

As the night wore on, Mary listened as the guests talked about the miracle that they had witnessed. She heard their disbelief turn to faith, as they realized that something extraordinary had happened that night. She watched as Jesus smiled and talked with the guests, his quiet strength and his compassion filling the room.

And she knew then that her son was not just a man, but a savior - the one who had come to bring light to a dark world.

As the night drew to a close, Mary found herself surrounded by the guests. They asked her about her son, about his wisdom and his power. They asked her to tell them more about him, about his teachings and his miracles.

And Mary spoke, her words filled with love and pride. She spoke of the child that she had raised, of the young man who had grown into a leader. She spoke of the love and the compassion that he had shown to all those around him, and of the hope that he had brought to the world.

And as she spoke, she knew that she was doing what she had been sent to do - to bear witness to her son, and to share his message of love and hope with the world; a world that so desperately needed it and would need it more in the future.

As she looked around the courtyard, Mary saw that the guests were moved by her words. They listened intently; their eyes fixed on her as she spoke. And she knew that her son's message was reaching them, touching their hearts and inspiring them to believe.

As the night came to an end, Mary watched as the guests slowly made their way out of the courtyard. She saw the joy and the wonder on their faces, and she knew that they would never forget what they had witnessed that night.

She turned to Jesus, who was standing nearby, his eyes closed in prayer. She smiled at him, knowing that he had done something truly extraordinary that night.

"Thank you, my son," she whispered. "Thank you for showing us your power and your love."

Jesus opened his eyes and looked at her, his face calm and serene. "It was nothing, Mom," he said. "My Father in heaven allows me to do anything I need to accomplish my mission. I just need to be careful. I want people to follow me and my teachings, not try to perform miraculous signs like changing water into wine. I did that out of love for you, mom. That is the essence of my mission – to show love to everyone. If people love freely, they love me."

Mary smiled at him, knowing that he was right. Her son was not just a man, but a messenger of God, sent to bring light, love and hope to a world that desperately needed it.

Mary knew that her life would never be the same again. She had witnessed something truly miraculous that night, and she knew that her son's message of love and hope would continue to spread, bringing light to the darkness and hope to the hopeless.

And she knew that she had been blessed to be a part of it all, to bear witness to her son's greatness and to share his message of love with the world.

Her Concern

From the moment he was born, Mary experienced a feeling of reverence and amazement at the child she had brought into the world. As he grew up, she watched him closely, always amazed by his wisdom and his compassion for others. When he began his ministry, she was both proud and concerned. She knew that Jesus had a message that the world needed to hear, but she also knew that his path would not be an easy one.

Mary watched as Jesus spoke to crowds of people, healing the sick and comforting the brokenhearted. She saw the joy on their faces and the hope in their hearts, and she knew that her son was doing something truly remarkable. But she also saw the fear and anger in the eyes of some of the religious leaders. They watched Jesus with suspicion, wondering who he really was and what he was trying to do.

One day, as Mary was walking through the streets of Jerusalem, she overheard a group of religious leaders talking about Jesus. They spoke in hushed tones, but Mary could sense their hostility. They accused Jesus of blasphemy and said that he was leading people astray. Mary's heart sank as she listened to their words of envy. She knew that Jesus was a good man, a holy man, but she also knew that there were those who would not accept him, nor his mission.

When Mary returned home, she found Jesus surrounded by a group of his disciples. They were all talking and laughing, and for a moment, Mary forgot her worries. She smiled at her son, but then she saw the exhaustion in his eyes. He had been working so hard, preaching and healing, and she could see that he was tired. Mary knew that she needed to speak to him, to share her concerns and offer him her support.

"Jesus," she said softly, "may I speak with you for a moment?"

Jesus looked up at his mother and smiled. "Of course, mom. What is on your mind?"

Mary took a deep breath and gathered her thoughts. She knew that she needed to be honest with her son, to tell him how much she loved him and how much she worried about him.

"I am so proud of you, Jesus," she began, "but I am also concerned. I hear the things that people are saying about you, and I worry for your safety. The religious leaders are angry with you, and I fear that they may try to harm you."

Jesus reached out and took his mother's hand. "I understand your concern, mom, but you must trust in my Father's Plan. I am doing the work that I was sent to do, and I will continue to do so, no matter what happens."

Mary nodded, tears welling up in her eyes. She knew that her son was right, that he was following a path that had been laid out for him. But it was hard to watch him suffer, to see the rejection and the hostility that he faced every day.

"I just wish that I could do something to protect you," she said, her voice barely above a whisper.

Jesus squeezed his mother's hand. "You can, mom. You can pray for me, and you can continue to support me as you always have. Your love and your faith give me strength, and I am grateful for them."

Mary smiled through her tears. She knew that her son was right, that her love and her faith were the most powerful weapons she had. She would continue to pray for him, to support him, and to love him with all her heart.

As Mary left the room, she felt a sense of peace. She knew that her son was in God's hands, and that he would be protected and guided as he continued his ministry. She could hear the sounds of the city outside, the hustle and bustle of people going about their daily lives. She could smell the aroma of spices and incense that wafted through the air. But in her heart, she knew that there was something else, something deeper and more profound, something that she could not quite put into words.

It was a sense of connection, a feeling of being part of something greater than herself. She had always felt this way, ever since the day that the angel had appeared to her and told her that she would bear a son. But now, as she watched her son go out into the world and share his message of love and hope, that feeling was stronger than ever.

Mary knew that her son was not just her son; he was a light from God, a teacher and a healer who had come to show people the way to the kingdom of heaven. And she knew that even if his path was difficult, even if he faced rejection and persecution, he would continue to do what he believed was right.

Mount Tabor

Mary sat anxiously in the shade of a large oak tree, waiting for Peter, James, and John to return from their journey up Mount Tabor. She knew that something significant had occurred, and she couldn't wait to hear all about it.

As the three men approached, Mary could see that they were glowing with excitement. They were animatedly speaking to each other, their gestures wide and expressive. Mary stood up to greet them, her heart beating faster with anticipation.

"Welcome back," she said, smiling at them.

Peter, James, and John grinned in unison as they approached her. "Mother Mary, you won't believe what we just experienced," Peter said, his eyes wide with wonder.

"We saw Jesus transfigured before our very eyes," James added, his voice filled with awe.

Mary's heart skipped a beat. "What do you mean?" she asked, her eyes fixed on the three men.

"It's hard to describe," John said, shaking his head. "We were up on the mountain, and suddenly Jesus' face began to shine like the sun. His clothes became dazzling white, and then Moses and Elijah appeared and began to talk to him."

Mary felt a shiver run down her spine. "What did they talk about?" she asked.

"We couldn't hear everything, but they talked about Jesus' upcoming death and resurrection," Peter said, his eyes serious.

Mary felt a lump form in her throat. She knew that religious leaders had their feathers ruffled by Jesus' preaching and his actions, had no idea that their accusations of blasphemy would be strong enough to call for his death! Hearing it confirmed by her closest friends was almost too much to bear. "What else did you see?" she asked, her voice barely above a whisper.

"We saw a bright cloud come down and cover us," James said, a hint of wonder in his voice. "And then we heard a voice from the cloud saying, 'This is my beloved Son, with whom I am well pleased; listen to him.'"

Mary felt tears well up in her eyes. She knew that this experience was something special, something divine. "What did Jesus say about all of this?" she asked.

"He told us not to tell anyone what we saw until after he had risen from the dead," Peter said, his brow furrowed with concern.

Mary felt a pang of confusion. Why would Jesus want them to keep something so amazing a secret? "But why?" she asked.

"He said that people wouldn't understand until after he had risen," John said, his voice soft. "He said that we needed to wait until the time was right."

Mary nodded slowly, trying to understand. She knew that Jesus was wise, but this seemed like such an incredible event that it was hard to keep quiet about it. "Did he say when the right time would be?" she asked.

"He didn't give us a specific time," Peter said, his eyes scanning the horizon. "But he did tell us that we would know when the time was right to share what we saw."

Mary felt a sense of relief wash over her. She trusted Jesus implicitly, and if he said that they needed to keep this a secret for a while, then she knew that there must be a good reason. "I understand," she said, smiling at the three men. "Thank you for telling me about your experience."

Peter, James, and John nodded in unison, their faces filled with a sudden feeling of awakening. Mary watched as they walked away, their steps lighter than before, but also knowing that they just didn't recognize the magnitude of the act that Jesus would have to suffer an agonizing death before he could rise from the dead. She knew that this experience had changed them, had given them a glimpse of the divine that few people ever got to see.

As Mary sat under the oak tree, lost in thought, she suddenly felt a hand on her shoulder. She looked up to see Jesus standing over her, his face filled with compassion.

"Hello, Mom," he said, his voice soft.

"Jesus," Mary said, smiling up at him. "I heard about what happened on the mountain. It sounds like it was an incredible experience."

"It was," Jesus said, sitting down next to her. "But it was also a difficult one."

Mary felt a sense of concern wash over her, then she put her arm around him, hugging him close to her like she did when he was a child. "I think I know why" she responded.

"I had to prepare my closest friends for what was to come," Jesus said, his voice serious. "I knew that they needed to see me in my glory, to understand that even though I would suffer and die, I was still the Son of God."

Mary felt a sense of sadness wash over her. She knew that Jesus' journey would not be an easy one, that he would face incredible hardship and pain. "I'm so sorry, Jesus. This is the mission we both were asked to do. We will be sharing the pain" she said, her voice barely above a whisper.

She knew that time was running out, that soon he would be taken from her. She looked into his eyes and saw the pain and sadness there, but also a sense of calm and acceptance. She knew he was prepared for what was to come, but as his mother, she couldn't help but feel a deep ache in her heart.

"Jesus, my son," she said softly, "I want to tell you something that has been weighing heavily on my mind since the day of your presentation at the temple."

Jesus looked at her, his eyes full of love and concern. "What is it, Mother?"

"It was Simeon," Mary said, her voice barely above a whisper. "Simeon was a devout and righteous man who was eagerly awaiting the coming of the Messiah. The Holy Spirit had revealed to him that he would not die until he had seen the Lord's Christ." She continued.

"He said something to me, something that has stayed with me all these years," Mary said, her voice shaking slightly. "He said that a sword would pierce my soul. At the time, I didn't understand what he meant, but now I do. I understand all too well."

Jesus took her hand and held it tightly. "I know, Mom. I know that this is hard for you. But it is all part of my Father's Plan."

"I know that," Mary said, tears streaming down her face. "But it doesn't make it any easier. I wish I could spare you from all of this. I wish I could keep you safe and protect you from harm."

"I know you do, Mother," Jesus said, his voice full of compassion. "But you must trust in God's plan. Everything happens for a reason, even the things that we don't understand or that seem unfair."

Mary nodded; her heart heavy with grief. She knew that Jesus was right, that she needed to have faith and trust in God the Father's plan. But it was hard to let go of her fears and worries, especially when she knew that her son was facing such a difficult and painful path.

As she sat there with Jesus, holding his hand and listening to his words of comfort and wisdom, Mary felt a sense of peace wash over her. She knew that she couldn't change what was to come, but she could take comfort in the fact that her son was strong, brave, and filled with love and compassion.

In that moment, Mary made a decision to focus on the present, to cherish every moment she had left with Jesus, and to trust in God's plan for their lives. She knew that it wouldn't be easy, that there would be many more tears and moments of pain and sorrow to come. But she also knew that with faith and love, they would make it through.

Journey to Jerusalem

Mary watched as Jesus and his disciples made their way south toward Jerusalem from the safety of Galilee. She could feel the tension in the air as they neared the city, knowing that something was about to happen. As they reached the base of the hill, Jesus stopped and turned to his followers.

She could see the weariness in his eyes, the weight of the task he had been given seeming to bear down on him. Yet despite his exhaustion, his voice was strong and steady as he spoke.

"Listen to me carefully," he said, his eyes scanning the faces of those gathered around him. "We are going up to Jerusalem, and the Son of Man will be delivered over to the chief priests and the teachers of the law. They will condemn him to death and will hand him over to the Gentiles to be mocked and flogged and crucified."

Mary felt a lump form in her throat as she listened to her son's words. She knew that what he was saying was true, and her heart ached at the thought of the suffering he would have to endure.

But Jesus wasn't finished yet. He continued, "On the third day he will be raised to life!"

Mary felt a great consolation ignite in her chest at his words. Despite the darkness that was to come, there was still light on the other side. But She knew that her son's message was not an easy one to hear. He was telling them that he would have to endure pain and suffering, that he would be mocked and scorned, and that he would die a humiliating death on a cross. But even as he spoke these words, Mary could see that the apostles did not fully understand the gravity of what he was saying.

They still held on to the belief that Jesus would enter Jerusalem as a victorious king, that he would overthrow the Roman occupiers and establish a new kingdom. They did not want to believe that their beloved teacher and leader would have to endure such hardship and suffering.

She watched as Jesus turned to his disciples and said, "Whoever wants to be first must be your slave—just as the Son of Man did not come to be served, but to serve, and to give his life as a ransom for many."

As Jesus finished speaking, the disciples began to murmur amongst themselves, jostling for position and trying to figure out who would be the greatest in the kingdom. The apostles still did not understand! They argued among themselves, jockeying for positions of power and authority in the coming kingdom. They seemed more concerned with their own status and position than with the message that Jesus was trying to impart.

But Mary knew that Jesus had already answered that question. It wasn't about greatness or power or prestige. It was about service and sacrifice and love.

As they continued on their journey up to Jerusalem, Mary walked alongside her son, her heart heavy with both sadness and pride. She knew that what lay ahead would be difficult, but she also knew that Jesus was doing what he had been called to do, and that was something to be celebrated.

Temple Entrance

Mary was a woman of deep faith and profound understanding. She knew that her son had a mission that was for a great purpose. But now, as she watched Jesus enter the temple in Jerusalem and drive out the money changers and merchants, she felt a mixture of pride, concern, and awe.

She knew that Jesus was capable of great things, but she had never seen him act with such force and determination. The sight of him overturning tables and driving out the merchants with a whip filled her with concern. She knew that her son was fulfilling the prophecies of the Messiah, but she also feared that these actions targeted the wrong people.

By driving out the money changers and sellers of temple sacrifices, Jesus was making a statement about the true purpose of the temple, and the need to respect and honor the sacred space. His actions were also a criticism of the religious leaders of the time, who were not fulfilling their duty to protect the sanctity of the temple.

As she watched Jesus, she felt a tap on her shoulder. Turning around, she saw one of the disciples, Matthew, standing behind her.

"Mother Mary," he said, "may I speak with you for a moment?"

"Of course, Matthew," Mary said, turning to face him.

"I wanted to talk to you about what we just witnessed," Matthew said, gesturing towards Jesus as he continued to drive out the merchants. "I'm not sure I fully understand why he's doing this. I mean,

I know it's written in the scriptures that the temple should be a house of prayer, but why is Jesus so angry?"

Mary paused for a moment, considering her words carefully. She knew that the disciples were still struggling to fully understand the true nature of Jesus' mission, and she wanted to help them see the deeper meaning behind his actions.

"Matthew," she said, "do you remember the story of when Jesus was a boy and we lost him in Jerusalem?"

Matthew nodded, and Mary continued. "When we found him in the temple, he said to us, 'Did you not know that I must be in my Father's house?'"

"Yes, I remember that," Matthew said.

"Well, the temple is the house of God," Mary explained. "And Jesus is here now, as the Son of God, to fulfill the prophecies and to bring about the kingdom of God. But the people in the temple have turned it into a marketplace, a place of commerce and greed. Jesus is angry because they are defiling the house of God and dishonoring his Father."

Matthew nodded, but Mary could see that he was still struggling to fully grasp the concept. "But why does Jesus need to be so forceful?" he asked. "Why can't he just preach and teach, like he usually does?"

Mary sighed. She knew that this was a difficult concept for the disciples to understand. They had grown accustomed to Jesus' gentle and compassionate nature, and they were not yet ready to see him as the powerful and righteous judge that he truly was.

"Matthew," she said, placing a gentle hand on his shoulder. "Jesus is both the Lamb of God and the Lion of Judah. He came to bring salvation to the world, but he also came to judge the unrighteous and to cleanse the temple. He is acting out of love and righteousness, and his actions are necessary to fulfill his mission."

Matthew nodded, his eyes wide with understanding. "I see," he said. "Thank you, Mother Mary. You always have a way of helping us see things more clearly."

Mary smiled warmly at him. "It is my pleasure, Matthew. I am always here to help you and the other disciples understand the true nature of Jesus' mission."

As she turned back to observe Jesus, she felt proud that he was being so forceful, as sometimes you have to stand up for what you believe is right. She knew that her son was doing the work of God, and that he was fulfilling his divine purpose. She also knew that he was facing great danger and opposition, but she had faith that God would protect him and guide him on his path.

As Jesus continued to drive out the money changers and merchants, the temple began to fill with people who had been watching from outside. Many of them were amazed and inspired by Jesus' actions, and they began to gather around him, eager to hear what he had to say.

Mary watched as Jesus spoke to the crowd, his voice strong and clear. She could see the passion and conviction in his eyes, and she felt a deep sense of awe and reverence. She knew that her son was not just a teacher or a prophet, but the very Son of God.

As the day wore on, Jesus continued to teach and preach, healing those who were sick and lame, drawing more and more people to him. Mary knew that her son was fulfilling his destiny and bringing hope and salvation to the world.

As the sun began to set, Jesus and his disciples left the temple and made their way back to the home of their friend Joseph, from Arimathea. As they walked, Mary could sense that something was troubling Jesus.

"Is everything alright, my son?" she asked, placing a hand on his arm.

Jesus sighed deeply. "I am troubled, Mom," he said. "I know that the time is coming when I must suffer and die. The religious leaders and the Roman authorities are conspiring against me, and I know my life remaining is short."

Mary felt a pang of fear and sadness in her heart. She knew that her son was facing great danger, and she longed to protect him from harm, as she and Joseph did after the magi left.

"Jesus, my son," she said, her voice trembling. "I know that your path is difficult and full of challenges. But I also know that you are doing the work of God the Father, and that He will guide you on your journey until your mission is complete."

Jesus smiled at her, his eyes full of love and gratitude. "Thank you, Mom," he said. "Your faith and your love give me strength and courage."

The Last Supper

As Mary watched Jesus move from disciple to disciple, washing their feet with such tenderness and care, her heart swelled with love and admiration for her son. She saw the dirt and grime that had accumulated on their feet from walking the dusty roads of Jerusalem and the calluses that had formed from years of hard work. Yet, Jesus did not shy away from the messiness of their lives, but rather embraced it with open arms. As he poured water over their feet and dried them with a towel, Mary could feel the love and humility radiating from him.

She watched as Peter protested, refusing to let Jesus wash his feet, but Jesus gently reminded him that he must serve others just as he had served them. Mary knew that this act of service was a reminder that they must love and care for all those whom God loved, including the dirty, the homeless, those in prison, the ill and the lame, the poor as well as the rich. Jesus wanted his disciples to understand that God the Father loved them all and he would allow that love to be displayed through the next 24 hours.

She watched as the first cup was mixed with water and wine, the Cup of Sanctification, and as the father began with the formal blessing over the cup. The food was then brought out, including unleavened bread, bitter herbs, a bowl of sauce, and the roasted lamb, which was known as "the body" in traditional Jewish sources, although the actual meal had not yet started.

The aroma of the roasted lamb filled her nostrils, and the flickering of the candles cast a warm glow over the faces of those gathered around the table. She could hear the sound of their voices mingling together in prayer and song, and the clink of the cups and plates as they were passed from hand to hand.

Mary watched with a heavy heart as Jesus continued to speak, his words piercing her soul. She knew that he was referring to Judas, the disciple who had always been a bit of an enigma, quietly seething with anger and resentment. She could see the tension between Jesus and Judas, and the way he avoided Jesus' gaze. Mary knew that this was the one who would betray her son.

As Jesus revealed that one of them would betray him, Mary's heart filled with anxiety. Her mind raced, trying to make sense of what was happening. She couldn't believe that one of their own could do such a thing. Yet, she could see the guilt and shame etched on Judas' face, as he shifted uncomfortably in his seat.

When Jesus told Judas to go and do what he had to, Mary's heart sank and the mood in the room shifted. Mary watched in horror as Judas rose from the table and made his way to the door. She could see the fear and anxiety on his face as he left the room, and she knew in that moment that he was going to betray her son. She knew that this would be the beginning of the end for her son. She watched as the other disciples looked around in confusion and fear, not understanding what was happening.

Mary continued to listen as the third cup, the Cup of Blessing, was mixed, and the supper officially began. They ate the lamb and the unleavened bread, with a blessing over the bread, and then Jesus broke the bread and shared the cup of blessing as his own Body, Blood, Soul, and Divinity. He commanded them that they were to do the same in remembrance of him, making him the sacrificial lamb of God in atonement for our sins.

As the fourth cup, the Cup of Praise, was not prepared, Mary listened intently to the voices of the disciples as they began to sing the Hallel Psalms. She could hear the melody of Psalm 115, where King David wrote, "We will bless the Lord from this time forth and forevermore. Praise the Lord!" The lyrics brought tears to Mary's eyes as she knew that her son, Jesus, would soon give the ultimate sacrifice for humanity's sins.

She then heard the words of Psalm 116, where David wrote, "I love the Lord because he has heard my voice and my pleas for mercy. Because he inclined his ear to me, therefore I will call on him as long as I live." Mary knew that these words spoke to the importance of prayer and how it connected people to God. It reminded her of the strength that Jesus found in prayer and the comfort that it provided him.

As the disciples continued to sing, Mary heard the words of Psalm 118, where David wrote, "The stone that the builders rejected has become the cornerstone. This is the Lord's doing; it is marvelous in our eyes." Mary realized that these words were a prophecy about her son, Jesus, and how he would be rejected by the religious leaders and the people. But she also knew that he would become the cornerstone of the Christian faith, the foundation upon which it would be built.

The Hallel Psalms brought a sense of calm to Mary's heart, even in the face of the upcoming torture and death of her beloved son. She knew that Jesus' sacrifice was part of God's plan and that it would ultimately bring salvation to humanity. As the disciples finished singing, Mary felt a sense of gratitude for her son and the message he brought to the world.

As the meal drew to a close and Jesus and the disciples left in the darkness for the Mount of Olives, Mary felt a sense of peace settle over her. She knew that her son's mission was coming to its climax, and she was filled with a sense of awe and wonder at his perfect timing. She knew that he was the one who had come to save the world, and that he would do so in his own way and in his own time.

The Arrest

Mary had been sleeping fitfully when she heard the news. She had been tossing and turning all night, her mind filled with worry and concern for her son. She knew that he was in danger, that the authorities were seeking to arrest him, and she had spent the night praying for his safety.

But now, as the first rays of dawn began to filter through her window, she heard a knock at her door. She sat up in bed, her heart racing with fear.

"Who is it?" she called out, her voice trembling.

"It's John," came the reply. "Mother Mary, you need to come with me. They've arrested Jesus."

Mary felt a wave of panic wash over her. She had known that this day would soon come and he had known that her son's teachings and recent actions would upset the authorities. But now that it was happening, she felt a sense of overwhelming sadness and despair.

She quickly got dressed and followed John out into the street. The city was buzzing with activity, people rushing back and forth, their faces filled with fear and uncertainty.

Mary felt a sense of dread wash over her. She knew that her son was in their custody, and she knew that they would do everything in their power to make sure that he never walked free again.

John knew that they took Jesus to Annas' palace first, where the Sanhedrin hastily met and held their "trial". After that, they brought him across the Kidron Valley to secure him at Caiaphas' House. John told Mary that Peter had gone ahead to determine what they were planning to do with Jesus.

John said "Mary, please hold my hand and we will head out of the Golden Gate". The hill down the valley was steep and rocky, so they had to be careful not to fall. Once they crossed over, the climb up the Mount of Olives was very steep and equally rocky. They finally got to the steps leading up toward Caiaphas' House. It was there, on the steps, they met with Peter.

Peter's face was dirtied with the fine dust that swirled through the valley in the morning sun. He had streaks from tears dripping down to his chin. He cried uncontrollably as he gabbed Mary's hand. Peter said "Mother, how can you ever forgive me". She said "Peter, what could you have done?". He said "Mother, I denied Him... Not just once, or twice, but three times". "How can you ever forgive me?", he continued.

Mary said "Oh Peter, we all fear pain and suffering of our witness to the truth. You have had little sleep my son. Jesus taught forgiveness for the last three years, why do you think he would stop now?" Mary continued "now go to Joseph's house and meet the others in the upper room".

John and Mary continued up the steps that seemed to never step. Once they got to the courtyard only a few people stood around the charcoal fire warming their hands. The smell of the courtyard was overwhelming. The stench of sweat mixed with the dust and dirt of the ground, making it hard to breathe. Mary could also smell the smoke from the fires the soldiers had lit, which added to the suffocating atmosphere. She closed her eyes, taking a deep breath to try and calm herself, but the smells only seemed to get stronger.

There were a couple dozen people on the pathway from the courtyard to the front of Caiaphas' house. The crowd started making raising a racket and held their fists as they shouted. Mary and John could see the red tops of the soldier's crest popping up above the crowd as they pushed their way through.

Mary felt a wave of despair wash over her as she pushed her way through the soldiers until she saw two of them dragging Jesus through the crowd. Once the two saw Mary, they dropped his nearly lifeless body on the cobblestone walkway. She could see the bruises on her son's face, the blood on his clothes, and she knew that he had been beaten and tortured.

She knelt down next to him, her heart breaking. "Jesus," she whispered, her voice choked with tears. "What have they done to you?"

Jesus looked up at her, his eyes filled with pain. "Mother," he said, his voice soft. "I'm so sorry."

Mary felt a sense of confusion wash over her. "Sorry?" she asked, her voice barely above a whisper.

"I knew that this day would come," Jesus said, his voice filled with resignation. "But I never wanted to put you through this."

Mary felt a wave of sadness wash over her. She knew that Jesus had a greater purpose, a greater mission, but she couldn't bear to see him suffer. "I love you," she said, her voice filled with emotion.

Jesus smiled weakly; his eyes filled with love. "I love you too, Mother," he said. "And I want you to know that what I'm doing is for the greater good. I'm doing my Father's Will."

Mary nodded slowly, trying to understand and ignore the soldiers and crowd. She knew that Jesus was special, that he had a mission, but it was hard to see him in so much pain. "What can I do?" she asked, her voice pleading.

"Just be strong," Jesus said, his voice barely above a whisper. "Pray for me, and pray for those who have done this to me. And know that I will always be with you, even if I'm not physically here."

Mary nodded, her heart breaking. She knew that she had to be strong, that she had to keep her faith in God and in her son. But it was hard to see him in so much pain, to know that he would soon be gone from her life.

As the soldiers prepared to take Jesus away, Mary stood up, her eyes fixed on her son. She knew that this was not the end, that there was still hope for him, for their people, for the world. But it was hard to see that hope through the tears in her eyes.

She watched as they led him away, her heart heavy. She knew that this was just the beginning of a long and difficult journey, one that would test her faith, her strength, and her love for her son. But she was determined to see it through, to stand by her son no matter what happened.

As the soldiers disappeared into the distance, Mary and John knelt down on the ground, their eyes closed in prayer. They prayed for strength, for courage, for hope. Mary prayed for her son, for his safety, for his mission, for his love.

And as she prayed, she felt a sense of peace wash over her. She knew that she was not alone, that God the Father was with her, and that her son was doing the work of God. And she knew that no matter what happened, she would always love him, always stand by him, and always believe in him.

The Sentence

Their prayer continued for Jesus to remain strong until His mission was complete. Then they knew they should get to the Praetorium where they would need to get Pontius Pilate to declare the sentence on Jesus. The steep steps back down the hill slowed down their path back across the Kidron Valley and back up to the Golden Gate.

Mary and John stood in the packed Praetorium Courtyard, their hearts heavy with grief and fear. Mary's eyes scanned the crowd, looking for the familiar faces of Jesus' followers, but all she saw were strangers. The rising morning sun was blazing down on them, making the air hot and dry. Mary wiped the sweat from her forehead, her eyes never leaving her son, who stood before the steps to Pilate's throne, surrounded by soldiers.

The sounds around her were chaotic. The murmurs of the crowd grew louder with every passing moment, and Mary could hear the clanking of armor and weapons as the soldiers moved around her son. The shouts of the soldiers as they barked orders to the people around them echoed in her ears. Mary could also hear the whispers of the Pharisees and the Sadducees, who had plotted against Jesus for so long. They were working the crowd, trying to get a sentence of death by crucifixion.

Mary's eyes opened as she saw her son being pushed and pulled by the soldiers. They were taunting Him, laughing at Him, and spitting on Him. Mary's heart broke as she saw the bruises on His face, the blood trickling down His cheek from where one of the soldiers had hit Him with the back of his hand.

Mary wanted to rush forward and protect her son, to take Him in her arms and shield Him from the cruelty of the soldiers. But she knew that she couldn't. She had to stay strong, to watch as her son faced His accusers and be judged.

The sight before her was a nightmare. Her son, the son she had raised, the son she had nurtured, was being accused of blasphemy, and she knew what the penalty was. Mary listened as the high priest answered Pilate's questions, watched as Jesus remained silent, knowing that He had done nothing wrong. Mary could sense the fear in His eyes, the uncertainty of what was to come.

The trial continued for what seemed like hours, with Mary watching in silence. She could hear the jeers of the crowd growing louder, could see the Pharisees and Sadducees whispering among themselves. Mary knew that they were plotting against her son, trying to find a way to condemn Him to death.

As the trial came to an end, Mary's heart sank. Her son had been found guilty, condemned to death by crucifixion. Mary could hear the cheers of the crowd, the soldiers laughing and joking as they prepared to take Jesus away. She wanted to scream, to protest, but she knew that it was pointless. Her son had been judged, and there was nothing she could do to save Him.

Pontius Pilate, the Roman governor of Judea, ordered Jesus to be scourged as a form of punishment before deciding His fate. Pilate hoped that the brutal beating would satisfy the bloodlust of the religious leaders who sought Jesus' execution, and perhaps even persuade them to spare His life.

Mary watched in horror as her son was stripped, tied to a post, and scourged by the Roman soldiers. She could hear the sickening sound of the whip as it lashed against His flesh, each blow leaving behind a trail of blood and torn skin. The stench of sweat, fear, and blood hung heavy in the air, mixing with the sounds of the soldiers' shouts and the gasps and cries of onlookers.

Mary's heart broke with every strike of the whip, with every scream of agony that came from her son's lips. She wanted to rush forward, to shield Him from the punishment, but she knew that there was nothing she could do. She watched in horror as the soldiers beat Jesus until His skin was raw and His body was covered in blood.

The sight was almost too much to bear, and yet Mary could not look away. She knew that her son was innocent, and yet He was being subjected to such brutality. She felt a deep sense of helplessness, of frustration and anger at the injustice of it all. She wished He would end it all right there. What more would He have to do to prove that He was the Son of God the Father?

Mary's ability to stay with her son and witness His scourging was a testament to her faith and her unwavering devotion to God's will. As a mother, it must have been an unimaginably painful experience to watch her son being tortured and humiliated in such a brutal way. But she knew that Jesus had come to earth for a purpose, and that purpose was to save humanity from their sins.

She had watched Him grow into a wise and compassionate young man, teaching others about God's love and mercy. And even though she must have known that this path would be difficult and painful, she remained steadfast in her support of Him.

As Jesus was being scourged, Mary would have been filled with a range of emotions - anger at the injustice of it all, sadness at seeing her son suffer, and a deep sense of helplessness. But she also knew that this was all part of God's plan, and that Jesus had willingly taken on this burden to redeem humanity.

Mary's faith in God's plan allowed her to endure the pain and suffering of her son's scourging. She must have drawn strength from her belief that Jesus was fulfilling His mission to bring salvation to all who believed in Him. And in her heart, she must have known that her own sacrifice - the sacrifice of watching her son suffer and die - was a small price to pay for the greater good.

Through it all, Mary remained a source of strength and encouragement for her son. She was there to offer Him comfort and support, to remind Him of His purpose, and to hold His hand as He endured the pain and humiliation of His scourging.

Mary's unwavering faith and devotion are an inspiration to all who seek to follow in the footsteps of Jesus. Her ability to endure such pain and suffering, while remaining steadfast in her support of her son, is a testament to the power of love and the strength

Finally, the scourging ended, and the soldiers unbound Jesus from the post. Mary rushed to her son's side, trying to offer Him comfort and solace, even as He struggled to stand. She could see the deep wounds on His back and the blood that soaked through His tunic, and her heart ached with the knowledge that there was nothing she could do to ease His pain.

She watched as Jesus was taken away to be presented to the crowds, His body broken and battered, but His spirit unbroken. Mary felt a sense of both pride and despair as she watched her son stand tall, even in the face of such cruelty.

As Jesus was presented to the crowd, Mary could hear the jeers and taunts of the people, the shouts of "Crucify Him!" ringing in her ears. She could see the hatred and anger in their eyes, and she knew that they were blinded by their own fears and prejudices.

Through Mary's eyes, the trial and scourging of Jesus were a devastating experience, one that left her heartbroken and shaken to her core. But even in the face of such darkness, she held onto her faith, knowing that her son was destined for greatness and that His sacrifice would ultimately bring hope and redemption to all who believed.

As Mary stood in the courtyard, watching as her son was taken away, she knew that she would never be the same. Her world had been turned upside down, her heart shattered into a million pieces. But even in the face of such overwhelming grief, Mary knew that she had to stay strong. She had to be there for her son, to support Him in any way that she could.

Mary's love for her son was unbreakable, and even in the face of His impending death, she knew that she would always stand by His side. The trial may have condemned Jesus to death, but it could never break the bond between mother and son.

Mary followed the soldiers as they led Jesus through the winding streets of Jerusalem, the hot sun beating down on their backs. The crowd grew thicker as they made their way towards Golgotha, the place where Jesus would be crucified. Mary could hear the wails and cries of the people around her, the sound of mourning and despair filling the air. She knew that their despair would soon be turned into joy, on the day of His Resurrection. But she dreaded the event that was about to take place.

The smell of death was heavy in the air as they arrived at the place of execution. Mary could see the crosses already set up, the wood rough and splintered. Her heart ached as she watched the soldiers begin to prepare her son for His death. They stripped Him of His clothes, leaving Him completely naked and exposed to the elements, as a way to humiliate him further. Mary could see the wounds on His back, the bruises on His arms and legs. She wanted to run to Him, to hold Him and comfort Him, but the soldiers kept her back.

Mary watched in silence as her son was nailed to the cross, His body wracked with pain. She could hear the sound of the hammer hitting the nails, the smell of blood filling her nostrils. Her heart felt like it was breaking with every passing moment, her tears flowing freely down her cheeks.

The sound of her son's voice broke through the chaos, a voice filled with pain and love. "Father, forgive them, for they know not what they do." Mary could hear the desperation in His voice, the plea for mercy. She wanted to comfort Him, to tell Him that everything would be alright, but she knew that it was too late. As she stood there, she prayed to God the Father to not let him suffer much longer. She heard some behind her laughing and saying that if he truly was the son of God to order the angels to come down and remove him from the cross, as if it were the evil one tempting him all over again on one last ditch effort to fight good with his evil.

Every drop of blood that fell to the ground sounded like thunder when it hit the dried dirt. Mary saw the blood of her son running in four directions, one to the north, one to the south, one to the east and one to the west and was reminded of Ezekiel 47:8-12 she memorized as a young girl

"This water flows toward the eastern region and goes down into the Arabah, where it enters the Sea. When it empties into the Sea, the water there becomes fresh. Swarms of living creatures will live wherever the river flows. There will be large numbers of fish, because this water flows there and makes the salt water fresh; so where the river flows everything will live. Fishermen will stand along the shore; from En Gedi to En Eglaim there will be places for spreading nets. The fish will be of many kinds—like the fish of the Great Sea. But the swamps and marshes will not become fresh; they will be left for salt. Fruit trees of all kinds will grow on both banks of the river. Their leaves will not wither, nor will their fruit fail. Every month they will bear, because the water from the sanctuary flows to them. Their fruit will serve for food and their leaves for healing."

This reminder of the outcome yet to be revealed of the saving power as a result of her son's pain, suffering and death gave her a wave of strength as she prepared to see him take his last breaths.

And as she stood at the foot of the cross, watching her son suffer and die, Mary knew that his sacrifice had not been in vain. His message of love and compassion had touched the hearts of countless people, and his example of humility and sacrifice had inspired generations of believers.

But even as she held on to this hope, Mary could not help but feel a sense of sadness and disappointment. She had seen firsthand how difficult it was for the apostles to understand the gravity of what Jesus had come to do. She knew that they had failed to fully grasp the depth of his sacrifice, and that they had clung to their own ideas of power and glory rather than embracing his message of love and service.

But even in the midst of her disappointment, Mary held on to her faith and her love for her son. She knew that his sacrifice had changed the world forever, and that his message of love and compassion would continue to inspire and guide humanity for generations to come.

As Mary stood before the cross and watched her son die, she remembered the visitation of the Magi and the gifts they had brought. She remembered the gold, a symbol of royalty and kingship, the frankincense, a symbol of divinity and prayer, and the myrrh, a symbol of sacrifice and burial.

And as she mourned the loss of her son, she would draw comfort from the knowledge that his life had been touched by the divine, and that his death was not the end, but only the beginning of something greater.

The minutes passed in a blur, the sun slowly sinking towards the horizon. Mary stood at the foot of the cross, her heart heavy with grief. She watched as her son's breathing became more labored, His body growing weaker with every passing moment. The sounds around her grew quieter, the smells of death and despair overwhelming. And then Jesus cried out with a loud voice, "Father, into thy hands I commend my spirit" and having said thus, he gave up his Spirit.

It was over. Mary watched as her son's body went limp.

As the feast of Passover was celebrated, the soldiers took His body down from the cross, and Mary fell to her knees in grief. She could hear the sound of her own sobs echoing through the air, could feel the weight of her loss crushing her.

The Passion of Jesus had come to an end, but Mary's pain would never go away. The sights, sounds, and smells of that day would be with her for the rest of her life, a constant reminder of the love and sacrifice of her son. But even in the face of such overwhelming sorrow, Mary knew that she would always love Jesus, and that He would always love her.

The Tomb

Together with a few of Jesus' followers, Mary made her way to the tomb of Joseph of Arimathea, a place of rest that had been hewn from the rock cliffs of Golgotha. The journey with His body seemed long but she was determined to see her son laid to rest with dignity and respect.

When they arrived at the tomb, Mary helped to prepare Jesus' body for burial, washing it clean and anointing it with oils and spices. It was a painful task, but she knew that it was necessary to honor his memory and show him the love and respect that he deserved.

As they laid Jesus' body to rest, Mary stood beside the tomb, her heart heavy with grief. But even as she mourned, she could feel a sense of peace settling over her. She knew that her son's death had not been in vain, that it had been a necessary sacrifice for the greater good.

And so, as she gazed out over the rolling hills of Golgotha, she found herself speaking words of hope and encouragement to those around her. She urged them not to despair, not to give up hope, even in the darkest of times.

"For my son," she said, "gave his life so that we might all have hope. He knew that his sacrifice was necessary for the salvation of all mankind. And so, we must not give up hope, even in the darkest of times. For there is always a light at the end of the tunnel, a glimmer of hope that shines even in the darkest of places."

Mary's words were like a balm to those around her, offering comfort and reassurance in a time of great uncertainty. And even as she mourned the loss of her son, she knew that he was watching over her, guiding her and giving her the strength to carry on.

For Mary, the death of her son was not the end. It was the beginning of a new era, one in which hope and love would prevail. And as she stood there, watching over his tomb, she knew that his legacy would live on, inspiring generations to come with the message of love and hope that he had preached during his time on earth.

The Resurrection

Mary awoke before dawn on the third day after the crucifixion of her son, Jesus. She had hardly slept, consumed with a combination of hopefulness mixed with grief and despair. As she laid there, she thought about making her way through the darkened streets of Jerusalem towards the tomb where Jesus had been laid to rest, to meet up with Mary Magdalene, Mary the mother of James and Salome. They had made plans to further anoint His body. But Mary's heart was heavy with sorrow and she just stayed there praying.

Mary's mind kept wandering to visions of when she stood at the foot of the cross when her son had breathed his last breath. She remembered how she had felt the weight of his body as it was taken down from the cross and carried to the tomb. The memory of his lifeless form haunted her, and she felt as though a part of her had died with him.

But even in the depths of her grief, Mary held onto a glimmer of hope. She remembered the words of her son, that he would rise again on the third day. It was a promise that seemed too good to be true, but Mary had faith that her son was the Messiah, the Son of God, and that he would keep his word.

Across town, at the tomb, the three women could see that the stone had been rolled away from the entrance. Their hearts began to race with anticipation, and they ran towards the opening, desperate to know what had happened.

Inside the tomb, Mary Magdalene, Salome and the other Mary saw that the burial cloths had been left behind, but there was no sign of Jesus. They felt a sudden surge of energy coursing through their bodies, as if a bolt of lightning had struck them. They knew in their hearts that something incredible had happened.

As the started to walk out of the tomb, suddenly, they saw a figure standing behind them. It was Jesus, alive and radiant, just as he had promised. Mary Magdalene fell to her knees, tears of joy streaming down her face, as she realized that Jesus had indeed risen from the dead. He was alive, just as he had promised, and he had conquered sin and death with his sacrifice on the cross!

Mary Magdalene looked up at him, her heart overflowing with love and gratitude, as she reached out to embrace him, but Jesus told her not to cling onto Him. It was a moment of pure joy, as Mary Magdalene Jame's mother Mary and Salome stood there in amazement, and they knew that the world would never be the same again.

Jesus spoke to them, telling them to go and tell the Mary His mother and the disciples what had happened. They obeyed, running through the streets of Jerusalem to tell the others.

Meanwhile, the disciples were gathered together in a room, afraid and uncertain of what the future held. They had seen their beloved leader die on the cross, and they were afraid that they would be next.

When Mary arrived at the upper room, the other disciples were already there, huddled together and talking in hushed tones. They were still in shock over what had happened, and Mary could see the grief etched on their faces. She was relieved to be among them, but she was also filled with a sense of anticipation that she couldn't explain.

But then, the women running from the tomb pounded on the doors and when opened, they burst into the room, breathless with excitement, and told them what had happened. Her heart was bursting with happiness, joy, and jubilation, all of which were evident on her radiant face.

As she watched, Jesus appeared before the disciples, and Mary's heart swelled with hope. She had always believed in her son's promise of eternal life, but seeing him alive and well after his crucifixion and death filled her with an unshakable faith. The sight of Jesus standing before his disciples, his wounds visible but healed, was the most beautiful thing Mary had ever seen.

Mary gasped in shock and stumbled back a few steps. It was him. She could feel it with every fiber of her being. Her son, the one who had been crucified and buried, was standing right there in front of her, alive and whole.

Tears of happiness streamed down her cheeks as she watched her son speak to the disciples. She listened intently as he explained the scriptures, which had prophesied his death and resurrection. Mary had always known that her son was special, but this moment reaffirmed her belief that he was the Son of God, the savior of the world. But a part of her was afraid that if she got too close, he would disappear.

As the disciples gathered around Jesus, Mary noticed that some of them also were still hesitant, unsure if they should believe in what they were seeing. She understood their doubts and fears, having experienced them herself when she first learned of Jesus' fate. With a gentle smile, Mary stepped forward and spoke to the disciples, encouraging them to have faith in Jesus and his promise of eternal life.

"Believe in him," Mary said, her voice filled with love and compassion. "He is the Son of God, the light of the world. He has conquered death, and his love for us will never fade. Trust in him, and you will find peace and eternal life."

The disciples listened to Mary's words, and slowly but surely, their doubts began to fade. They saw the joy and happiness in Mary's face, and they felt the same emotions swelling within their own hearts. They looked at Jesus, who smiled back at them, and they knew that what they were seeing was real.

Mary's words of encouragement had given them the strength to believe, and they felt a renewed sense of hope for the future. They knew that with Jesus by their side, they could face any challenge that lay ahead.

As the disciples continued to speak with Jesus, Mary stepped back, her heart overflowing with gratitude and happiness. She looked up at the sky, marveling at the beauty of the world around her. She knew that her son's resurrection was a miracle, and she felt blessed to have been a witness to it. Mary watched in awe as her son interacted with the others, smiling and speaking in his familiar voice.

She closed her eyes and whispered a prayer of thanks, thanking God for his mercy and love. She prayed for all those who had yet to believe, asking that they too would see the truth and find hope in Jesus' resurrection.

Mary opened her eyes, and as she looked at the disciples gathered around Jesus, she felt a sense of peace and contentment that she had never experienced before. She knew that her son had fulfilled his mission, and that his message of love and salvation would continue to spread throughout the world.

Jesus seemed to sense his mom's need for a hug. Their eyes met, and Mary felt a jolt of recognition shoot through her. This was her son, but it was also so much more. He was the risen Lord, the Savior of the world. Mary fell to her knees, tears streaming down her face, as Jesus walked over to her.

He knelt down beside her, and she could feel his hand on her shoulder. It was warm and solid, and she knew that it was really him. She looked up at him, and he smiled at her. It was a smile that she would never forget. It was filled with love, and joy, and peace. It was the smile of her son, but it was also the smile of her Savior.

For a few moments, they just looked at each other, and Mary felt as though the rest of the world had fallen away. There was only her, and her son, and the love that they shared. And then, slowly, Jesus reached out his hand to her. She took it, and he helped her to her feet.

They stood there for a few moments, just holding hands and looking at each other. Mary could feel the tears running down her face, but she didn't care. She was filled with a sense of wonder and gratitude that she had never felt before. She knew that everything was going to be alright. Jesus had risen from the dead, and nothing would ever be the same again.

The disciples were overjoyed, and they went out into the world to spread the good news of the Resurrection. They preached in the streets, in the synagogues, and in the homes of the people, telling everyone they met about the miracle that had occurred.

For Mary, the Resurrection of Jesus was a moment of incredible joy and hope. It was a moment that would forever change the world and bring salvation to all who believed in her son's sacrifice. As she looked back on that day, Mary knew that her faith had been strengthened, and that she would always be grateful for the miracle of her son's ministry, and the impact he had on the world.

As the days passed, Mary watched as her son continued to appear to his disciples, teaching them and guiding them as they spread the good news of his resurrection. She saw the hope and joy that he brought to people's lives, and she knew that her son's sacrifice had not been in vain.

Mary also saw the impact that her son's resurrection had on the world. People who had been lost and without hope were now finding new purpose and meaning in life. They were inspired by Jesus' message of love and forgiveness, and they began to live their lives in a new way, guided by the teachings of the Messiah.

As the days went by, Mary watched her son's ministry continue to unfold, and she witnessed his disciples spreading the message of his resurrection with unwavering fervor and without fear. She saw the joy and hope that he brought to people's lives, and she felt a profound sense of pride and gratitude for her son's selfless sacrifice.

As she saw the impact of her son's resurrection on the world, she felt a sense of awe and wonder. People who were once lost and hopeless were now finding new meaning and purpose in their lives. They were inspired by Jesus' message of love and forgiveness, and they began to live their lives in a new way, guided by the teachings of the Messiah.

Pentecost

Mary sat quietly in the upper room with the disciples, waiting patiently for the arrival of the Holy Spirit. She could feel the excitement building inside her as she thought about what was to come. She had been a faithful follower of Jesus since the beginning and had witnessed his crucifixion and resurrection. She knew that this was a pivotal moment in the history of the early church community.

As she looked around the room, she saw the fear and uncertainty in the eyes of some of the disciples. They had been through so much together and had faced so many challenges. Mary understood their doubts and fears, but she also knew that they needed to have faith in the promise of eternal life that Jesus had given them.

As the disciples continued to pray and wait, Mary felt a warmth spreading through her body. She knew that this was the Holy Spirit arriving, just as Jesus had promised. The disciples began to speak in different tongues, and Mary felt a surge of joy and happiness within her.

She stood up and began to speak to the disciples, her voice filled with hope and encouragement. "My dear friends," she said, "do not be afraid. The Holy Spirit has come to us, just as Jesus promised. We must have faith in the Lord and believe in the promise of eternal life that he has given us."

Mary's words had an immediate impact on the disciples. They began to feel a renewed sense of hope and joy, and their fear began to dissipate. They knew that Mary had always been a pillar of strength and faith, and her words gave them the courage they needed to face the challenges ahead.

As the day of Pentecost continued, Mary witnessed an awe-inspiring sight that shook her to her very core: the disciples, filled with the Holy Spirit, fearlessly pursued the mission of spreading the good news of Jesus Christ to all they encountered. Through their fiery preaching and unyielding devotion, they baptized thousands of people into the faith, undeterred by the persecution and rejection that they encountered. Mary marveled at their unshakable faith and steadfastness in the face of adversity, knowing that they drew their strength and guidance from the Holy Spirit. Their fearless pursuit of spreading the gospel filled Mary with a visceral sense of awe and wonder, inspiring her to join them in their mission to bring salvation and hope to all those who would hear the message.

Mary saw firsthand how her son's teachings transformed people's lives. They were no longer bound by the constraints of their past mistakes or the negativity of the world around them. They found solace in the knowledge that they were loved and forgiven, and they embraced their newfound freedom with open hearts and minds.

One day, Mary witnessed a man who had been paralyzed for years rise from his bed and walk, his body now healed by the power of her son's teachings. She saw the tears of joy in the man's eyes, and she knew that her son's impact on the world was far-reaching and profound.

She also saw how her son's message of love and forgiveness challenged the societal norms of the time. People who were once shunned by society were now accepted and embraced as equals, and Mary felt a sense of hope for a world where everyone was treated with dignity and respect.

Despite the many challenges that her son's ministry faced, Mary knew that his teachings would endure. She saw how the message of his resurrection had spread across the world, touching the lives of countless individuals who had been searching for something to believe in.

In the end, Mary felt a sense of peace and fulfillment, knowing that her son's sacrifice had brought hope and healing to a broken world. She knew that his legacy would live on, inspiring generations to come with his message of love, forgiveness, and redemption.

To those who may be scared to believe in Jesus and the promise of eternal life, Mary would say that there is nothing to fear. God's love is infinite, and he has a plan for each of us, a plan that will big us happiness and fulfillment. If we trust in him and follow his teachings, we can find peace and joy that will last for eternity.

And if you feel unworthy of His love, remember that God loves you just as you are. He sees the beauty in you, and he has a plan for your life that is uniquely yours.

So have faith, my friends. Trust in God's plan, and know that he is always with you, guiding you every step of the way. And remember that the promise of eternal life is real, and that it is available to all who believe in Jesus Christ, repents and draws closer to him and draw others to Him.

Gabriel's words were filled with hope and promise, and he explained that the Holy Spirit would come upon her. That child Mary would bear would be called the Son of God. She felt a sense of peace wash over her as She listened to him, and She knew that She had to trust in God's plan for her.

My own experience is proof of this. Though She faced many challenges and difficulties along the way, She never lost my sense of hope and faith in God. And She knows that the same is true for anyone who puts their trust in him.

God bless you on your journey!

Don't miss out!

Visit the website below and you can sign up to receive emails whenever John H Brennan publishes a new book. There's no charge and no obligation.

https://books2read.com/r/B-A-KVCX-OIVGC

BOOKS 2 READ

Connecting independent readers to independent writers.

Also by John H Brennan

Thru The First Disciple's Eyes
Thru the First Disciple's Eyes

Standalone
Advice From Above

About the Author

John is a cradle Catholic, the middle child of five, who grew up in upstate New York. Vatican Two saved him from learning Latin the year he trained to be an Altar Server. He attended Catholic School until High School when he transitioned to public school. He received two associates degrees from the local Community College, then started a job in a fortune 500 company as a draftsman. He had met the woman of his dreams and they had the first of their children 9 months after they were married. Six months later, the three headed off to the State University of New York at Buffalo where John studied Mechanical Engineering. By the time John graduated with his BS in Mechanical Engineering, they had their second son and headed back to his hometown to continue his 40 year career and have a third son and finally his daughter. He and his wife now have a son in law, a daughter in law and six beautiful grandchildren. Several events led him to deepen his faith – joining a Catholic Men's Bible Study; attending several Catholic Men's Conferences; attending a Catholic Men's Emmaus Retreat as well as being on several Emmaus Retreat Teams (including giving witness talks); attending daily Mass; Praying the Holy Rosary daily and being an Extraordinary Minister of Holy Communion at Church and Nursing Homes in the area. His engineering job brought him across the USA as well as Mexico, Europe and Asia where he enjoyed creating his own personal Pilgrimages to Holy Sites and sharing the experiences and pictures with family and friends. His retirement ambitions include enjoying his children and grandchildren, continued travel to holy sites around the world and sharing his Catholic faith wherever he can.